T0358494

# STUDIES ON INDUSTRIAL PRODUCTIVITY: SELECTED WORKS

Volume 2

# WHY NATIONS PUT TO SEA

# WHY NATIONS PUT TO SEA

Technology and the Changing Character of
Sea Power in the Twenty-First Century

KEVIN L. FALK

Routledge
Taylor & Francis Group

LONDON AND NEW YORK

First published in 2000 by Garland Publishing Inc.

This edition first published in 2019
by Routledge
2 Park Square, Milton Park, Abingdon, Oxon OX14 4RN

and by Routledge
711 Third Avenue, New York, NY 10017

*Routledge is an imprint of the Taylor & Francis Group, an informa business*

*British Library Cataloguing in Publication Data*
A catalogue record for this book is available from the British Library

ISBN: 978-1-138-61548-9 (Set)
ISBN: 978-0-429-44077-9 (Set) (ebk)
ISBN: 978-1-138-32287-5 (Volume 2) (hbk)
ISBN: 978-0-429-45100-3 (Volume 2) (ebk)

**Publisher's Note**
The publisher has gone to great lengths to ensure the quality of this reprint but points out that some imperfections in the original copies may be apparent.

**Disclaimer**
The publisher has made every effort to trace copyright holders and would welcome correspondence from those they have been unable to trace.

# WHY NATIONS PUT TO SEA

## TECHNOLOGY AND THE CHANGING CHARACTER OF SEA POWER IN THE TWENTY-FIRST CENTURY

KEVIN L. FALK

GARLAND PUBLISHING, Inc.
A MEMBER OF THE TAYLOR & FRANCIS GROUP
NEW YORK & LONDON / 2000

Published in 2000 by
Garland Publishing Inc.
A member of the Taylor & Francis Group
29 West 35th Street
New York, NY 10001

10   9   8   7   6   5   4   3   2   1

**Library of Congress Cataloging-in-Publication Data**

Falk, Kevin L.
    Why nations put to sea  :  technology and the changing character of
sea power in the twenty-first century  /  Kevin L. Falk.
        p.    cm. — (Garland studies in industrial productivity)
    Includes bibliographical references (p.    )
    ISBN 0-8153-3527-X (alk. paper)
    1. Sea-power—Forecasting.    2. Twenty-first century — Forecasts.
I. Title.    II. Series: Garland studies on industrial productivity.
V25.F35    1999
359—dc21                                                        99-31319
                                                                    CIP

Printed on acid-free, 250-year-life paper
Manufactured in the United States of America

*For Marcia, my wife and best friend.*

# Contents

# Foreword

Doctor Kevin Falk describes here the relation between technology and the exercise of sea power. Besides illuminating that relationship, he reminds us of a neglected fact: the United States is a maritime nation whose interests and welfare depend on the successful exercise of sea power. That is, access to the sea, to the air above the sea, and to the depths beneath the sea serve the prosperity and safety of the general citizenry of the Republic, and that access is dependent on the exercise of sea power.

For the United States, sea power is an expression of the capability to control the maritime approaches to North America, to render safe and useful the arteries of commerce between North America and abroad, and to keep open those lines of communication that render possible material support for friendly nations whose safety is a vital interest of the United States.

Without control of the air, sea, and undersea approaches to North America; without the freedom to use the arteries of commerce; and without the capability to provide material support to friendly nations abroad, the United States cannot in wartime engage abroad those enemies who otherwise would bring the war directly to North America. It is the capability to apply sea power in the transoceanic world that makes a nation more than merely one with maritime interests.

Japan, Norway, the United Kingdom, and Italy all are maritime nations to a considerable degree. Yet none of those today has the capability to control its sea approaches, by itself, save in peacetime when no other nation contests that control. Their more distant maritime interests are only safeguarded, if at all, at the pleasure and for the convenience of other powers.

It is not well remembered that the British North American colonies were founded with the support of British sea power. It was British sea power that finally facilitated the driving out of France from the Ohio and Mississippi valleys in the French and Indian Wars. It was the maritime assistance of France that helped defeat British forces fighting against the American Army in the Revolution.

American labor laid the foundation for the country as a commercial republic, and American enterprise extended the commerce across the globe. After the Revolution, it was ships of the U.S. Navy that helped secure respect for the American flag and the ships and persons sheltered beneath it. In three wars—the Quasi-War with France, the Barbary Wars, and the War of 1812—freedom of the seas for American commerce was at the heart of the struggles.

American naval forces blockaded the Southern Confederacy isolating the American Civil War from European intervention, and thus helped prevent the breakup of the Union. Indeed, every war in which the United States became engaged with a European or Asian power was a war fought at sea and by sea, from the Revolutionary War through the Spanish-American War and the many wars of the twentieth century.

It is therefore ironic that we should, here at the end of the twentieth century, have all but forgotten that the United States has been a great maritime nation whose safety and prosperity depend on the ability to exercise sea power. The most prominent West Coast newspaper has offices within 16-inch gun range of the Pacific Ocean and nearly in view of the two great Pacific ports of Los Angeles and Long Beach, ports that handle thousands of tons of seaborne cargo daily. Yet the newspaper carries the outlook, in its columns, of landsmen who have never smelled the sea and have no concept of the United States as a maritime nation or of California as a place whose prosperity depends on seaborne trade. They might just as well live in Topeka, Kansas, for all the interest they manifest in things maritime. It is hardly better with most prominent U. S. newspapers, all of which are both careless and unknowing of the connection between the United States and the seas that environ it on three sides.

All this is symptomatic of our general loss of touch with the maritime interests of the United States. That loss of touch breeds a fatal ignorance bearing on the fate of the Republic. For having forgotten the necessity to exercise sea power, if we and our friends are to enjoy the freedom to use the seas, we become captive to the pleasures of those who still understand the importance of maritime endeavors and the exercise of sea power.

As Doctor Falk instructs us, technology makes the exercise of sea power possible. The mastery of technology and its generous application to the means of exercising sea power must be a constant endeavor whether in peacetime or wartime. In peacetime Americans have most often behaved as though they had all the time in the world—time to do all of those things that should have been done when there was time enough. They have taken their maritime interests lightly, and only when the crises come do they remember that their defense depends on naval forces conducting maritime strategy.

In 1937, the third of three joint congressional resolutions signed by the president, known as the Neutrality Act, was put into force. Our fleet had close to 1,000 ships of all types, some in operation and some in mothballs. Who would have imagined, let alone spoken publicly, that within seven years the fleet would require 66,000 vessels (of which all but 1,000 or so would have to be constructed between 1940 and 1944) if the United States and its allies were to win the war that the Neutrality Act was designed to keep us from. What good fortune for the Republic that, despite peace, naval disarmament, and budget balancing between 1918 and 1939, there were nevertheless those faceless beings in obscure facilities trying with limited funds to develop the technologies of radio optics, fire control, high explosives, submarines, gunnery, communications, electric welding, aeronautics, and all the other things that would make the naval forces of 1944 more effective than those of 1918.

Sea power may from time to time, in the euphoria of imagined peace, be forgotten as a necessity of state, but technology has a life of its own, multiplying, elaborating, and extending as though logarithmic. As Doctor Falk suggests, failure to advance the tools and instruments of sea power at the same pace as technological development is to render the maritime forces of this Republic impotent to protect the interests of the United States and therefore its strategic capability to wage war abroad. Since war will come in the normal course of events anyway, the ability to wage it abroad rather than in North America is crucial to the survival of this Republic.

Dr. Harold W. Rood
Professor of Government,
Claremont McKenna College

# Preface

This book maintains that the character and application of sea power will change in the next century due to transformations in technological innovation. Research conclusions suggest that organizational responses to technological innovation are decisive in sustaining modern armed forces. These "organizations" may be military, governmental, industrial, or a combination of the three. Indeed, within a given nation, various organizations may be working at cross-purposes with regard to the incorporation of advanced technology into the nation's armed forces. In summary, organizational responses to technological innovation varies; organizational responses to technological innovation matters.

The changing character of maritime power is evaluated through an examination of current trends, historical precedent, and deductive logic. Of the many factors influencing maritime power, an exponential growth in mankind's use of science and technology is the key to understanding the future of sea power. To a greater degree than has historically been true, a small number of states excelling in science and technology, and possessing the industrial capability to capitalize on that excellence, are distancing themselves economically and militarily from the mass of the international community. Within this small group of states, technological breakthroughs will enable states to leapfrog one another in power rankings (both in actual and in perceived rankings). Relative economic and military strength has never been a more fragile and waning national attribute. Since history offers examples both of ready acceptance of new technology and of organizational complacency in the face of change, the ability of national leadership to foster receptive attitudes toward technology within important government organizations will be of singular importance in the coming technological struggle.

Due to technological innovations the character of sea power may evolve into something much like that of traditional land power. This research demonstrates that those who suggest that maritime power is becoming irrelevant to modern international power rankings fail to understand the true nature of maritime power, or its historic resilience.

# Acknowledgments

This book is an adaptation of the dissertation that I completed in my doctoral studies at the Claremont Graduate University. It has been my pleasure to have Professor Harold Rood, Professor P. Edward Haley, and Professor David Arase oversee this research project. These gentlemen guided my graduate studies at the Claremont Graduate University, supported me throughout the qualifying examination process, and were instrumental in my formation of a viable dissertation plan. While I take full responsibility for any academic shortcomings this book may have, I gladly share credit with my dissertation committee for any effective expression of ideas contained in the following pages. I also wish to thank Gwen Williams and Sandra Seymour for their tireless work and immense support. These ladies, both staff members at the Claremont Graduate University's Department of Politics and Policy, readily demonstrate the fact that quality department staff members are essential to any graduate student's success. This dissertation is the result of years of study in foreign and defense policy. I owe a debt of gratitude to many people who have made this work possible—far too many people to thank each person individually at this time. To all of my family and friends who helped me through my graduate school years, my sincere thanks.

Kevin L. Falk, March 1999

# WHY NATIONS
# PUT TO SEA

# Introduction

## TOPIC AND RESEARCH PROBLEM

This research addresses transformations in the character and application of sea power. The phrases "sea power" and "maritime power" are used interchangeably by the author and are broadly understood to be the sum of a nation's ability to impact political, military, and economic decisions on the world's oceans.[1] The transformations considered are brought about by technological innovation; or more specifically, by a change in the cumulative rate of technological innovation. Changes in the international political order and the quest by nations to secure natural resources are acknowledged as important influences on sea power. However, these influences remain a secondary interest of this research.

The world may well be on the threshold of an era in which nations fight to control ocean territory in the same way that they once fought to control territory on the land. In this struggle the marriage of space-based reconnaissance systems and information technology will give the naval forces of developed nations an unprecedented capability to monitor and control events on the ocean surface. However, mines, submarines, nuclear weapons, and inventions such as the underwater missile offer emerging maritime nations a number of ways to counter the advantages of established naval powers. The result of this evolution is that in the next century we can expect the application of sea power to more closely mimic the traditional application of land power.

This research suggests that organizational response to technological innovation is decisive in sustaining modern armed forces. "Organizations" may be military, governmental, industrial, or a combination of the three. Indeed, within a given nation, various organizations may be working at cross-purposes with regard to military force structure and the incorporation of advanced technologies. In summary, organizational response to technological innovation varies; organizational response to technological innovation will become decisive in political-military affairs.

The transformation of the nature of technological innovation and growing international dependence upon the resources of the sea are seen as being fundamentally interconnected; a significant change in either can seriously alter the way we should view the remaining factor. The key to this investigation is the illumination of the political-military impact of a change in the rate of technological innovation. Studies of the effects of emerging technologies have long been a feature of foreign and defense policy analysis; and indeed, such studies are important and have contributed to our understanding of the tools that statesmen seek to apply to the international system. This research departs from past studies by emphasizing the rate of technological innovation as an independent phenomena—this in place of the traditional investigation of specific innovations. If mankind's pace of technological innovation is increasing, then what are the ramifications for the future exercise of sea power?

At its essence, maritime power is about transportation. The unique characteristics of water offer transportation possibilities that are markedly different from those found on land or through the air. A floating ship displaces a volume of water that is of equal weight to the weight of the ship itself, either empty or fully loaded with cargo. Ships can be built on a very large scale because water is fairly heavy (where air is not); the weight of water is 64 lb. per cubic foot.[2] Transport by water remains, and will remain for the foreseeable future, highly practical. Indeed, transport by water remains the only economically sound method of delivery for many bulk items traded internationally. In strategic terms, large and heavy equipment for military forces is easier to move by sea than by land or air. In purely economic terms, sea transport remains the option of choice for commerce in heavy or bulk commodities.

The great empires of the seventeenth, eighteenth, nineteenth, and twentieth centuries cannot be adequately understood without a consideration of the naval and mercantile power that they were able to wield. Inexplicably, modern studies in international relations largely ignore the significance of sea power in the international system. Seaborne international commerce too easily becomes forgotten as a tool of state power. The influence of naval power is often dismissed as shrinking in significance (this dismissal is not surprising since the advantages of mercantile power have been forgotten). It is true that the exercise of naval power appeared to undergo a dramatic transformation during World War II as its historic form of the surface combatant gave way to the modern dominance of aircraft (and aircraft carriers) and submarines. In fact the transformation was well underway during World War I. Had the modern tools of sea power changed the essence of sea power forever? Or, had the merging of the aircraft and the submarine into naval operations done little to alter the strategic rationale that guides maritime power?

During the Cold War years the role that maritime power played within the grand strategy of the world's premier naval power, the United States, was often unclear. The possible uses and the practical utility of maritime power appeared questionable since the principal battlefield of a hypothetical World War III was assumed to be either 1) a conventional land campaign in Europe, where the Soviet Union and her allies enjoyed a significant numerical superiority, or 2) a global nuclear war in which surface fleets could not long survive. Either of these scenarios casts doubt on the utility of naval power. Was it possible to construct a scenario in which naval superiority would by itself offer victory?[3] For many it seemed that the age of maritime power was past, or at least in its twilight. The death knell for sea power was premature; the exercise of sea power is, and will continue to be for generations to come, important to international politics. Rather than being made obsolete by new technologies and political change, both the military and economic[4] components of maritime power have adapted remarkably to improved capabilities— sea power has in effect been reinvigorated as a component of national power in the late twentieth century.

Somewhat counter-intuitively, the rediscovery of sea power as a national tool may prove most problematic for those nations that have dominated maritime affairs throughout this century. As B. H. Liddell Hart so clearly reasons in *Defence of the West*, nothing breeds complacency quite like past success.[5] Are those who lead the United States so accustomed to thinking of America as the premier maritime power in the world that they have come to assume that this is a fixed condition of international relations?[6] No doubt there are nations that desire to contest American sea power at the earliest practical opportunity. Fortunately for the United States and its allies, few nations have the technological expertise and industrial infrastructure to compete effectively in this arena, whatever their desires. Thus the number of potential challengers will remain small. However, among these few states jockeying for position may become quite intense.

Before any form of national power can be successfully utilized for strategic purposes both the nature and character of that form of power must be properly understood by those who would wield that power. This is then an investigation of change: the changing character of sea power generally, and the changing character of naval power specifically. It must be remembered that the equation is ever in flux since nations seek to develop capabilities that will enable them to follow the policy options that they prefer. This change in capabilities works in the negative as well as the positive. Consider the United States' policy of diverting Soviet amphibious and naval strength with land threats during the Cold War. Containment sought to provide the Soviets with political and military land threats (primarily in Europe and with China) that would raise the relative strength of the US Navy and ultimately precipitate the collapse of the USSR.

## THE NATURE OF MARITIME POWER

It seems logical that before a useful examination of the modern character of maritime power can take place, one must identify the essential nature[7] of maritime power. The nature (or essence) of maritime power is highly stable, if not in fact timeless. By examining the strategic goals that maritime power can achieve we are able to better understand the nature of maritime power. Thus we see that at its core, maritime power is inherently tied to efforts to efficiently transport military forces or economic goods. Only a new scientific understanding of the realities of the physical world will change the nature of maritime power. The importance that sea powers have exercised over world history from before the *pax Romana* to the *pax Americana* serves to illuminate the future of sea power. But even as the essence for sea power remains unchanged, the tools for maritime endeavors are ever changing. It is problematic to determine a generic blend of merchant[8] and naval power that would be appropriate for all nations. The maritime requirements of states is varied—but what determines those different requirements? Resolving the issue requires identification of those economic and security matters that nations must address and then determining which needs must be/can be addressed by that particular nation with an application of sea power. For many states, the freedom to pursue those political, economic, and military actions deemed in their best interest rests at least in part upon an ability to engage successfully in naval warfare and sea-borne trade. An ability to harvest natural resources from the seas will become an increasingly significant aspect of national power.

Despite the varied strategic uses of maritime power, certain factors appear to be changing the character of maritime power for all nations.

## THE CHARACTER OF MARITIME POWER

Throughout most of history the character of maritime power[9] has been slow to change, though it has indeed changed under the appropriate circumstances—that such a change is at hand today is the central argument of this book. In many ways the potential near-term changes in the character of sea power could be far more important than those experienced earlier this century. Sir Peter Gretton notes that weapons like the aircraft and submarine are new weapons systems that merely upset the current "offensive vs. defensive" balance in naval warfare.[10] Rather than fundamentally altering the nature of sea power, these "defensive" weapons of the early Twentieth Century only pretend to do so; indeed, Gretton cautions readers to be on guard "lest a dominant" offensive weapon should emerge. Technological innovation, a profound change in the international political system, the hunt for new deposits of natural resources, and the current international economic system all may push further the transformation that the character of maritime power has undergone since World War II.

First, as the rate of scientific and technological advance increases exponentially, the stability and peace of the international system may suffer.[11] Slow and steady technological advance tends to favor the established industrial and military powers; unpredictable and rapid technological innovation lying within the grasp of numerous second-tier states[12] threatens the position of the established first-tier powers. A great military power today may be next year's has-been as the operational capabilities of a competitor nation passes it by. This potential could lead to serious instability in international power rankings (both true and perceived rankings). Instead of watching a rival state gain on their nation's position over a period of *decades*, policy makers may now have reason to fear a reversal of relative military position in mere months if an important technological innovation can be successfully incorporated into a military application.[13] The pressure to act quickly before a reversal is realized could become acute—such pressure may lead some governments to contemplate preemptive military action. Of course this technological issue is not limited to maritime power implications—all power issues of the future will be impacted by this development.

Second, international economic lifelines across the oceans are becoming more fragile than ever. Fewer cargo ships carry ever more goods across the oceans. Such trends suggest that a nation dependent upon sea-borne international trade will find its economic and industrial Achilles Heel ever more exposed. States dependent upon such trade will come to fear more than just declared war and the *guerre de course* that would surely follow such a declaration. A rogue nation with even a single competent submarine could wreak economic havoc upon the world economic system.[14] Worse still, in the short-term how could the other powers know which state (or terrorist group) to retaliate against? By their nature, submarines tend to make positive national identification difficult (though not impossible). Whether through declared war or covert intrigues, the vulnerability of nations dependent on sea-borne trade will only increase.

This research offers readers a conceptional framework of maritime power that should be of inter-disciplinary value. An application and merging of economics, history, and security studies is appropriate for a subject of this scope. There exists today a great conceptional divide between traditional and modern images of sea power. This divide is due in large part to the fact that easily seen instruments of sea power stopped looking like they used to after 1945. Because the maritime characteristics of the Cold War era saw many departures from the characteristics of proceeding eras of maritime power, many assumed that the strategic calculus of sea power had forever changed—or even that sea power had ceased being relevant altogether. The supposed division between traditional images and modern images of sea power is in one sense a real division and in another senses an overstated and mistaken concept. On the one hand a real change brought on by technological innovation has occurred; on the other hand, many of the timeless principles of naval strategy remain consistent with those known for centuries. Twentieth Century changes in the character of maritime power have been fundamentally evolutionary, rather than truly revolutionary. The true revolution in sea power, such as it is, is still on the horizon. Curiously, this "revolution" may well add to the political influence of maritime power more than it signals the obsolescence of this ancient form of power.

## RESEARCH ASSUMPTIONS AND METHOD

This research is grounded in neo-realist assumptions about the international system.[15] The basic thesis of this book is that maritime power (as a part of a nation's overall military and economic competition with other nations) has played and will continue to play a decisive role in the international system. Maritime power is seen as a necessary enabler, if not of itself a sufficient requirement, for economic, military, and, ultimately, for political power.[16] Flowing from this view is the belief that traditional tasks of maritime power have not been made obsolete by more modern forms of air power—in fact, new activities are likely to be added to traditional maritime tasks. Underlying this research will be the assumption that states seek the freedom of action to accomplish those things that suit their interests. To this end states will, if they are able, develop the political, economic, geographic, and military capabilities to ensure the greatest degree of freedom possible.[17]

No single research method was applied to this book—for example, the paper does not rely on formal modeling methods to validate or negate a hypothesis. It is my contention that an over reliance upon a particular method or paradigm blinds researchers from a true understanding of their question since any analysis that did not fit neatly into that methodological or conceptual box would have to be avoided. Instead, this is a study of the strategic characteristics of maritime power based largely upon history and logic. Unquestionably, my central argument that the character of maritime power will be significantly effected by changes in technology, the international political system, the availability of natural resources, and the international economic system, can be either discredited or supported by evidence that I discover. Thus my research is scientific and rigorous in the sense that I seek a true understanding of the traits and constitution of sea power.

## NOTES

1. I am not referring merely to naval and merchant vessels when I consider "maritime power." The concept speaks as much to the building blocks of maritime power as it does to its obvious manifestations. The components of sea power will be commented on in detail later.

2. See J. G. Crowther and R. Whiddington, *Science at War*, Philosophical Library, Inc., 1942, p. 151, for further details. These authors point out that if water weighed only half as much per cubic foot, then ship would have to build twice as large to carry the same load.

3. An import caveat to this was the expected value that nuclear-armed submarines would have in global nuclear combat. These vessels would not fight as traditional naval units; rather, they would hide in the depths until called upon to launch their missiles.

4. By "economic" I include trade, commerce, and commercial development of the oceans.

5. In Chapter XIX of *Defence of the West*, William Morrow & Co., 1950, Hart gives specific examples of this complacency in history, for example the interwar French Army's unwillingness to recognize the new armored warfare school: "The heads of the French Army were supremely convinced that they knew more about war than any other army in the world and were apt to despise all others except the Germans as amateurs. Although not 'too proud to fight' they were too proud to learn news ways of fighting" (218). The French attitude was not unique historically—documented examples of complacency being a plague to the successful exist dating back to the fall of Rome.

6. Is the United States the world's premier maritime power? The short answer appears to be: yes. America appears to have the most capable navy, and retains significant transport capabilities. However, since sea power is about transportation, declining American transport capabilities suggest that America's independent ability to conduct naval operations in distant waters is waning. Some suggest that "ownership of sea-borne transportation is misleading; they would instead investigate "access" to such transportation. This line of investigation assumes that access to foreign owned shipping during times of conflict will remain as they are during times of peace. As this paper will show, such an assumption is not warranted.

7. National power is understood to be the sum of political, military, and economic assets (tangible or intangible) that a nation may wield. Governments struggle to obtain a relatively high level of national power because they desire the wealth and freedom of action that they perceive is derived from such power. Though the tools of national power sometimes change, nations have long recognized what Colin Gray has termed the "strategic leverage" of sea power. In this understanding sea power is then one possible aspect of overall national power.

8. The word "mercantile" is used throughout this paper to pertain to international merchants or traders; thus the phrase mercantile power denotes trade power. The use of this word should not be confused with the political-economic philosophy of mercantilism.

9. By "character of maritime power" I refer to that combination of policy, strategy, tactics, weapons, and vessels that enable a state to achieve wealth and freedom of action in particular circumstances. The character of maritime power is thus ever-changing as new circumstances present themselves.

10. Gretton, Vice Admiral Sir Peter, *Maritime Strategy*, Frederick A. Praeger, Publishers, 1965.

11 The word "exponential" is not used in a mathematically rigid sense; my intention is to suggest that technological innovation seems to be increasing at an accelerating rate. The precise measure of that accelerated rate can not be known.

12. By "second tier states" I refer to successful, fully industrialized states that are not currently the dominant power in the area of interest. Thus the United

Kingdom and Peoples' Republic of China are both competent second tier maritime powers today, but both currently take a back seat to the dominance of American sea power. When discussing larger gaps between national capabilities such as those between France and Columbia, I will use "industrialized vs. non-industrialized" terminology.

13. The technological innovation may serve to revolutionize an existing weapon system, or it may lead to a new system altogether. One real world example lets us imagine a rival's navy suddenly being equipped with torpedoes that run at 50–60 knots instead of speeds at just under 35 knots. This rival navy is expecting its torpedoes to achieve speeds over 100 knots over the longer term. See "Why Not 100 Knots?," *Naval Institute Proceedings*, November 1996, for information on this Russian development. This very straightforward technological breakthrough, which enables the Russians to simply improve an existing weapon, effectively negates the anti-submarine doctrines of all western navies.

14. It is not that a single submarine could sink, by itself, a significant percentage of the world's shipping fleets. The danger would be found in the fear and uncertainty that such a warship could throw into the international financial system. Perceptions of economic vulnerability would likely be more significant than the actual threat.

15. This paper is not intended to build on the work of a specific realist or neo-realist theorist. As a means of understanding the international system, the basic belief system shared by realists is useful. The basic beliefs are understood to be: 1) the international system is a state—centric system wherein states jockey for position, 2) there is an assumption of rationality on the part of states, and 3) there is an assumption that states seek power to achieve their goals.

16. E. H. Carr in *The Twenty Years' Crisis: 1919–1939*, Harper Books, 1964, p. 108, states that political power can be divided into three categories: military power, economic power, and power over opinion (power over opinion is roughly used to represent the art of persuasion and propaganda). Carr claims that although these categories are theoretically separable, "it is difficult in practice to imagine a country for any length of time possessing one kind of power in isolation from the others." Maritime power can significantly affect a state's ability to make use of all three categories.

17. Geography can be "developed" in its own way. For example, strategically located territory can be acquired; this is evidenced in the modern era by new Chinese acquisitions in the South China Sea. Further, technology can be developed that better suits the geographic condition that a nation finds itself in.

# CHAPTER 1

# The Historic Importance
# of Sea Power

> *There is nothing—absolutely nothing—half so*
> *much worth doing as simply messing about in*
> *boats.*

> —KENNETH GRAHAME,
> *THE WIND IN THE WILLOWS*

## THE HISTORY OF SEA POWER

Men have gone to sea for all of recorded history. Initially the sea provided mankind with an abundant source of natural resources—especially food. There is ample archaeological evidence, such as fish bones found at the sites of ancient camps, to suggest that hunter-gatherers consumed fish. It is likely that early man caught what fish he could with his bare hands either from a riverbank or standing in shallow water near shore. This method of fishing apparently lasted for ages (and in a limited manner endures today). Archaeologists have found large numbers of harpoon tips and pointed fishing hooks in the camps of reindeer hunters of the Magdalene period, dating from sometime around 16,000 BC.[18] These finds appear to represent an improvement in fishing technology. The Magdalene hunters and gatherers evidently used all of the important fishing implements still being used today (fishing spear, hook, and net).[19] At first such implements would have been used from shore; it must have been only a matter of time before it was realized that greater catches of fish could be made in deeper water—thus the initial, and very practical, need that man go to sea. With the Magdalene hunter-gatherers we observe a dramatic leap forward in technology which leads to the re-organization of their society. The hunter-gatherer has become a fishermen—a historic transition rivaled only by the development of planned farming. Today mankind harvests 20 percent of its daily protein consumption from the oceans.[20] The radical technological advances of the plow and the hook have shaped modern social conditions. Future social conditions, evolving globally, may be shaped by the technological advances of our era.

Covering approximately 70 percent of the earth's surface, the oceans have a tremendous impact on global climate and weather. Extensive mineral and petroleum deposits, along with declining reserves of these resources on land, combine to make the oceans a significant and ever more important source of natural resources.[21] Man discovered long ago (the exact time frame has been lost in antiquity) the important idea that water supports weight as he gained experience on bodies of water while harvesting food.[22] The currents in rivers and streams provided locomotion at first, then paddles, poles, and oars were developed, later sails and steam were used. Mankind found then and still knows today that materials could be delivered quickly and more easily than by land across great distances by use of water. The eventual transport of valuable goods across the waters naturally led to piracy and warlike raids on rivers, lakes, and oceans; just as highway-men had long ambushed merchant caravans on remote roadways, so too would pirates ambush vessels in areas along popular shipping lanes.[23] As societies[24] began to appreciate the strategic value of what is now called "force projection" by water, the movement of troops across large bodies of water was realized. In some cases, seaborne piracy and looting actually became a common practice, as some communities made their living by piracy and sea-borne raids on settlements.[25] Piracy, troop shipments, and the clear military advantages of military force projected across water encouraged some governments to create sea-borne military forces.[26] As the historian F.E. Adcock explains, "naval warfare, in the strict sense, begins when ships not only carry men on warlike expeditions, but also are themselves instruments of war."[27] These naval forces were to protect friendly commerce by attacking those who would interfere with it.[28] The Phoenicians may have developed the first true naval vessels in about 700 BC. The Greeks, especially the Athenians, would later improve the design of the Phoenician galley; the basic Athenian galley design and their battle tactics dominated western naval warfare for about two thousand years.[29] Cultural legend springing from Homer's *Iliad* holds that Greek amphibious landings near Troy made possible the destruction of Troy during the Trojan War. Whether the Greeks truly "launched a thousand ships" in their war against Troy may never be known, but clearly without Greek naval supremacy to facilitate their troop landings there would have been no heroic siege.[30] The Greek historian Thucydides teaches that the Peloponnesian War was precipitated by Athenian domination of the Delian League.[31] The Delian League originally was intended to be a voluntary naval alliance, centered upon Athenian naval power, which would enable Greek city-states to resist the Persians. As the Persian threat receded the Athenians used the League as a vehicle to gain hegemony in Greece. Sparta was the only city-state still strong enough to attempt to check Athenian power. The Spartan victory over Athens in the Peloponnesian War owed in part to Sparta, a traditional land power, seizing supremacy of the sea from Athens. Lysander's destruction of the Athenian navy at Aegospotami in 405 BC effectively ended the war. Such success through the exercise of sea power is not unusual. The Roman victory over Carthage in the Second Punic War owed less to Scipio Africanus' victory over Hannibal at Zama in 202 BC than to the Roman command of the sea which contributed to the defeat of the great Carthaginian general on land.[32]

The exercise of sea power offers great utility in times of peace and war. In times of peace mercantile power is an important economic (and thus political) tool for nations. War ships can be used to demonstrate political will with friendly port calls or not-so-friendly displays of power. In times of war a merchant fleet marshals the resources of the world—both men and material. In times of war naval power guards friendly merchantmen while sinking or capturing enemy traders. If sufficiently powerful, naval power can be used to land troops in unexpected regions. During periods of conflict, sea power has provided its wielder with unparalleled strategic leverage.[33] For island and coastal nations, naval power is the first line of national defense. Beyond protecting home coastlines, sea power can equip and protect far-flung regions of interest from one's adversaries.

## GREAT SEA POWERS IN HISTORY

Many of the great empires of history were powerful, in part, because they based their power on applications of maritime power. The Phoenicians, Greeks, Romans, Portuguese, Spanish, Dutch, British, Japanese, and Americans could all be considered sea powers. Importantly, these states were very often successful in their rivalries with land powers. It is beyond the scope of this paper to comment in detail on the histories of all the great sea powers. Thus, the following summary is intended only as a modest reminder of the historic influence of sea power.

The Phoenicians were one of the earliest empires from which archeologists have discovered written records. It is apparent that the great wealth the Phoenicians accumulated was based upon their sea-borne trade. This trade was defended by the invention of naval forces. The original "sea power," the Phoenicians set the example for later maritime empires. Almost contemporaries with the Phoenicians, the Greek city-states are often thought of as a collection of small land powers—with the possible exception of Athens. Yet it was Greek naval power that thwarted the Persian Empires drive into Europe. The brave stand of Leonidas' Spartan garrison at Thermopylae was epic, but strategically indecisive. Less well known is the fact that this land battle was intended to bring about a naval battle on terms favorable to the Greeks.[34] Later in the conflict it was the naval battle at Salamis, on the flank of the Persian land advance, which led to the eventual defeat of the Persian expeditionary force in Greece. Denied supplies and reinforcements, the Persian army found its position untenable and it withdrew from Greece. Such success through sea power was not unique. The Romans have the classic attributes and outlook of a land power. And yet, the Romans used naval power to defeat their most serious challenger, the Carthaginians. Carthage was a sea power; to defeat Carthage in the Punic Wars, Rome became a sea power and eventually dominated the Mediterranean.

The advantages of sea power remain seen in contemporary times. In the past few centuries, the British held naval advantages first over the French, and later over the Germans. In their respective competitions with the English, the French and Germans both attempted to carry out both sea and land strategies. Conceding supremacy at sea to the British, both the French and Germans waged *guerre de course* on the British merchant fleet while pressing advantages on land. Ultimately, neither power achieved lasting success. In recent history, with the twilight of the British Empire, the United States largely has taken over the British maritime tradition. Maritime powers have been known to fail: The Japanese Far Eastern Co-Prosperity Sphere, based upon Japanese sea power, did not survive World War II. Interestingly it was a second maritime power, the Americans, who (along with naval forces of the British Common Wealth) defeated the Japanese.

## DEFINING SEA POWER

Sea power is a broad component of national power. Conceptually, sea power is often ambiguous; in this regard it is not unlike other components of national power that are so often described without precision. One would suppose that most individuals engaged in the formation of national security policy have a working understanding of the phrase "the exercise of sea power." Sadly, it is not always clear that those who write about of national security issues have a clear conception of maritime power.

For example, Alfred Mahan, while taking credit for coining the phrase "sea power,"[35] nonetheless failed to define it in any concise manner in either of his principal works, *The Influence of Sea Power Upon History* or *The Influence of Sea Power upon the French Revolution and Empire*. It is difficult to find a single definition of sea power in either classical or modern literature. The lack of an accepted definition of "sea power" is important in that it suggests a variety of useful approaches to the understanding of sea power. For the purposes of this paper, sea power will be considered to be that collection of military and other means that help define political, military, and economic relations among nations at sea.[36] This definition is necessarily broad since the modern components of sea power range from naval vessels to cargo ships, from aircraft production to deep-sea mining technology.

This wide range of categories reflects the components of sea power as contributing to: the capability to wage war on, over, under, and above the seas; the ability to conduct sea-borne commerce; the industrial base that can support both of these activities; and the technological facilities to extract useful materials from the sea itself. Brodie claims that sea power "has always meant the sum total of those weapons, installations, and geographic circumstances which enable a nation *to control transportation over the seas during wartime*" (italics in original).[37] This definition is no longer sufficient—though it remains an excellent description of sea power during times of war (when states are most susceptible to a loss of control over their sea-borne transportation). Beyond his neglect of the industrial-technological foundation of sea power, Brodie neglects any conception of the positive strategic effects that the exercise of sea power may have for a state during times of peace. We find then that rather than state what sea power is, many writers have chosen instead to emphasize what sea power does. It is as though the necessary broadness of a true definition of sea power renders "sea power" too large a subject for most writers. Colin Gray's excellent *The Leverage of Sea Power* is a case in point of this tradition—the literature informs as to the uses of sea power, but makes little attempt to define it.

Sea power, then, can then be understood as comprising aspects of both 1) naval power and 2) mercantile power.[38] Since some nations are either naval powers or mercantile powers, but not necessarily both, it is sometimes useful to be specific when identifying which type of sea power a given nation is. South Korea is an example of a significant mercantile power that few would consider to be more than a severely handicapped naval power. While a major player in commercial activities, South Korea has little means to protect its sea-borne commerce. Thus, South Korea must depend on a friendly naval power (in this case the United States) to defend South Korean interests.[39]

## SOURCES OF SEA POWER

In *The Influence of Sea Power Upon History*, Mahan identifies six elements of sea power that are still useful in modern discussions of sea power. Mahan's elements of sea power are:

    I.. Geographical Position
   II. Physical Conformation
  III. Extent of Territory
  IV. Number of Population
   V. National Character
  VI. Character of the Government40

Mahan rolled these elements into a prescription for the successful exercise of sea power. Many now suggest that Mahan's elements are no longer useful because they were more a contemporary reflection of national assertiveness through naval power than a series of timeless principles.[41] In short, Mahan is accused of mistaking nineteenth century aspirations for a deeper truth. It has been suggested that Mahan's six elements of sea power were in fact dated even as they were written, since Mahan's emphasis on a battle fleet (led by battleships) gaining control of the seas through decisive battle with the enemy fleet did not survive even World War I; this though he had written his work recently in 1894.[42] Crowl documents that even before the First World War many naval officers (particularly American officers) considered a reliance on historic battle tactics to be archaic. With such rapidly changing naval technology in the early twentieth century[43], could the tenets of naval power still be learned through a study of history? To his critics Mahan was engaging in a reactionary dependence upon history—worse still, this dependence was impractical in the face of new circumstances in which naval power would have to operate.[44] Many of the criticisms leveled at Mahan are unfounded. Mahan provides students of maritime power with an excellent starting point; a consideration of his six elements suggests the issues and attributes upon which a maritime strategists must first reflect. Additionally, Mahan's concept of a decisive battle by opposing battle fleets can be easily updated to reflect, for example, aircraft carriers instead of battleships. The Battle of Midway, albeit not fought by battleships, appears to be precisely the decisive fleet engagement that Mahan envisioned in his writing.[45] Nelson destroyed the combined French and Spanish fleet at Trafalgar—Nimitz destroyed the Japanese fleet at Midway. The different tactics used by the two commanders reflected the different capabilities of the vessels in their commands; importantly, the strategic effects were similar. The fact that modern states are able to compensate for deficiencies in any of Mahan's six elements to a higher degree than states of earlier eras does not invalidate a study of these six elements. Rather, the identification of those new national attributes that serve as effective substitutes for Mahan's six elements has replaced the study of the elements themselves.

The following diagram is useful when visualizing the components of sea power.[46]

**Sources**
A Maritime Community
Resources
Styles of Government
Geography
*Advanced Technologies Industries*
*International Political System*

**Elements**
Merchant shipping
Bases
The Fighting Instrument

**Effect**
Sea Power

Some of Mahan's "elements" have survived to be renamed as "sources" of maritime power in the above diagram. This change in terminology better reflects the true characteristics of the phenomena being studied.

## PRINCIPLES OF MILITARY POWER

Land warfare has numerous principles that historically govern its successful conduct. In Field Manual 100–5 the US Army distinguishes among three levels of war: military strategy, operational art, and tactics.[47] The US

Army then informs its officers that the dynamics of combat power are broken-down into maneuver, firepower, protection, and leadership.[48] Further, the US Army assumes that its ability to fight successfully depends on four basic tenets of land warfare: initiative, agility, depth, and synchronization.[49] Officers are evaluated during war games on the degree to which their plans have utilized these tenets of warfare, and the degree to which they show an appreciation of the dynamics of land warfare. Certainly the US Army recognizes that every combat situation is going to be unique. Past battles are studied today primarily to discern the reason for success or failure, and to understand the thought process of those who conducted the battle. Past battles are thus not studied with an eye to copying the disposition of forces; they are studied to determine whether or not the principles of war were correctly applied. While the US Army does retain "by-the-book" tactical solutions to common military problems, officers are encouraged to seek any workable solution to a problem after first demonstrating their grasp of officially sanctioned "school solutions." Even during Cold War fear of the Soviet land threat, AirLand Battle doctrine was intended to guide Army leaders, not restrict them.[50] Indeed, the only issue that the US Army seems doctrinaire about is the Army's official view of the deeper tenets and dynamics of land warfare—individual officers are not allowed to disagree with this official view. Thus in land warfare, as indicated by the doctrinal understandings of the United States Army, we find a developed understanding of the principals of warfare. What of the application of military power at sea? One would assume that the United States Navy would have an understanding of the tenets and dynamics of naval warfare that was as developed as the United States Army's concepts of land warfare. Remarkably, the Navy has no such common understanding of the basis of their form of warfare.[51]

A distinct American naval strategy did not exist as such before World War II, though individual doctrines, such as those guiding carrier operations or amphibious assaults, were under development.[52] As the Soviet naval threat became more serious in the late 1970s, the US Navy responded with the development of its Maritime Strategy.[53] Never as specific as the Army's AirLand Battle, the Navy's Maritime Strategy was more a collection of principles guiding coalition warfare at sea. Naval publications ". . . From the Sea," "Forward . . . From the Sea" and Naval Doctrine Publication 1 (NDP-1), *Naval Warfare*, represent recent attempts by the US Navy to further define strategies and doctrines for the use of naval forces in the furtherance of national policy. The task of establishing these doctrines has proven difficult; even the seminal commentators on naval affairs, individuals such as Alfred Mahan, found the principles of warfare at sea to be much more elusive than principles of land warfare.[54] Although recent naval publications claim to prepare "the Naval Service for the 21st Century," it seems that naval leaders are still struggling as they attempt to develop comprehensive principles of warfare.[55]

It can be argued in the generic sense that initiative, agility, depth and synchronization are the hallmarks of any successful military engagement; and in fact, these are all important ideas that naval officers are encouraged to heed. Does this imply then that naval warfare is fundamentally similar to land warfare? History suggests an understanding of one does not imply an understanding of the other. For example, Napoleon is highly regarded as a leader of armies; however, his reputation in warfare at sea is poor. Did Napoleon lack the maritime resources to deal effectively with the British Royal Navy, or did he misunderstand the appropriate application of sea power available to him? Unfortunately, there is no easy answer to this vital question. When considering Napoleon's naval resources, it is often pointed out that France and her allies (principally Spain) were able to form a combined fleet that was numerically superior to Nelson's ships at Trafalgar. This fact is no doubt important, but it is also deceptive. Despite the advantage of superiority in numbers, the combined French-Spanish fleet suffered greatly from a lack of effective joint training and joint doctrine. Further, the capabilities of the Spanish vessels and crews were questionable. During the battle French vessels initially followed traditional French hit-and-run naval tactics and attempted to outrun Nelson's ships. This tactic of choosing when and where to fight, and then disengaging the slower British vessels, had worked brilliantly for the French during naval engagements in the American War of Independence. However, slower Spanish vessels were unable to utilize this French tactic. Realizing that the Spanish vessels were not outrunning the British, French Admiral Villeneuve was placed in a difficult position: he could abandon the Spanish vessels (which surely would be defeated, and likely captured, by the British) or he could turn back and engage the British in a decisive battle (in which his combined fleet's superior numbers would be tested against the superior construction of British vessels). Villeneuve chose to fight, and Britain won a decisive victory. Most naval historians acknowledge the overall superiority of the British fleet at Trafalgar; even so, could Napoleon have done more with the ships he had? The vessels lost at Trafalgar might have been more usefully employed as a fleet-in-being. Did Napoleon err, or did he simply make a reasonable gamble and lose? On the balance most naval historians claim that Napoleon erred in allowing his fleet to sail. How could an acknowledged military genius make so fundamental a mistake? In the end we must conclude that Napoleon did not fully understand naval warfare. While broad similarities exist in all forms of warfare, crucial differences remain.

Where the elements of sea power may be ever changing, the usefulness of naval and mercantile power remains consistent. As an example, Till uses the following diagram to conceptualize the uses of naval power:[56]

**Means**
Fleet-in-Being
Blockade
Decisive Battle

**Effect**
Control of the Sea (limited)
Command of the Sea (never truly achieved,
     but approached

**Ends**
Coastal Tasks
Trade
Amphibious Assault
Naval Diplomacy
Strategic Deterrence

The order of events depicted in this diagram differs little today from what it has been in the past five centuries. Consider that the characteristics of a "decisive battle" have not changed through the centuries—it remains a battle that decides the outcome of an engagement, a set of operations, a campaign, or a war.[57] The tactical mechanics for achieving this victory have, obviously, undergone serious change (and will continue to change). Crossing the "T" as the Japanese did against the Russian Fleet at Tsushima in 1905 to gain a decisive victory was appropriate to engagements between formations of steam-driven armored ships whose weapons were great guns. The notion of crossing the "T" in today's world would be irrelevant to the mechanics of modern naval engagements. Nonetheless, while the look of naval battles has changed, the significance of decisive naval victories has not.

An inferior naval power unable to seek decisive battle can still influence the course of a naval campaign merely by keeping a competent combat force in play. The threat that such units may seek battle will likely force the superior force, not wishing to be defeated in detail, to mass its primary combat forces. Other units of the superior naval power may be assigned precautionary duties, such as convoy duty. Such massing of forces, or spreading out of forces on non-combat duties, keeps the superior force from prosecuting the war as effectively as it otherwise might. A modern example of this deployment occurred in the 1980s and 1990s; Middle Eastern states with modest naval power have used their gunboats to great effect in influencing the deployment of American warships. News that Iran may acquire even a single small submarine of limited range is cause for great concern among western navies.[58]

Lastly, blockades are still an important operation for naval powers. Containing an enemy force to proscribe its freedom of action may be part of a wider strategy at times. The blockade the United States imposed on Cuba was part of the policy of the United States against the Soviet Union. Though the American anger was with Soviet placement of missiles and bombers in the Western Hemisphere, the United States blockaded Cuba rather than the Soviet Union. The purpose of the blockade may suggest whether it is part of naval or maritime strategy in a war, or a way of carrying out a diplomatic policy without having to go to war. Cuba lacked the resources to break the blockade. The Soviet Union did not lack the resources to do so, but was not prepared to do so. On the other hand, the United States *at war* with North Vietnam did not impose a blockade (although it did lay mines in the approaches to Haiphong). It is through these means that control and command of the sea is won or contested.

## NAVIES IN THE NUCLEAR ERA

The development and deployment of nuclear weapons has presented the most important challenge to traditional visions of the principles of naval warfare. Is the classical understanding of naval warfare specifically, and sea power generally, made obsolete by nuclear weapons? Many writers on the subject of modern naval strategy say "no."[59] In fact, as the arm of the military force structure that stands the best chance to survive a nuclear strike, naval forces played a significant role in the war plans created by strategists during the Cold War era. Because navies by their nature are mobile, they do not provide an enemy with the hard-target reliability that army formations or land-based air force facilities offer.[60] An enemy can easily target naval port facilities, but the combat instrument itself is difficult to target when at sea. Nor is the role of navies in a nuclear exchange limited to merely hiding; in an offensive role, naval vessels (particularly submarines) provide a mobile and difficult to track, if expensive, nuclear platform. Aircraft carriers have long deployed aircraft that can carry and deliver nuclear bombs. Fleet air defense included in its arsenal the surface-to-air missile, starting with Talos (US) and Terrier (US), and evolving toward Standard-2 and beyond that could carry a nuclear warhead. Then there were surface-to-air weapons like the Tomahawk with a 200 Kt warhead. The Soviet Union deployed the surface-launched cruise missile SS-N-3 Shaddock in 1962 (with a 350 Kt war-head), the SS-N-T in 1968, the SS-N-9 Siren in 1968 (with a 200 Kt war-head), the SS-N-12 Sandbox in 1973 (with a 350 Kt war-head) and the SS-N-19 in 1980 (with a 500 Kt war-head). And of course none of these weapons equal the offensive power of submarine launched ballistic missiles like Polaris, Poseidon, or Trident (or similar Soviet strategic missiles).[61] With their mix of defensive and offensive nuclear capabilities, navies remain an important military component.

Why prepare for future battle at sea? After all, experience (expressed as a sort of conventional wisdom) suggests that the next great war will not be fought like the last one. Should we not then expect that the next major war fought between great nations will be an intercontinental missile exchange, or a battle fought in an exotic battlefield like space? While change is a major aspect of warfare, the underlying principles of land and sea warfare have remained virtually unchanged for centuries; much remains the same in military strategy even as technology quickly changes military tactics. Certainly the likely application of naval power during a war between two nuclear powers was forever changed by the July 1946 American atomic tests at Bikini Atoll in the Marshall Island chain. The magnitude of destruction inflicted by atomic weapons changed the manner of deployments of fleets. By demonstrating the ability of a single atomic weapon to cripple an entire combat fleet[62], the Bikini tests confirmed that changes in fleet deployment were necessary to successfully employ navies in wars against a nuclear weapon armed adversary. Although it can be argued that a post-Bikini Atoll flotilla will assemble *en masse* only at its own peril, it would be wrong to assume that naval power specifically, and maritime power generally, has thus become irrelevant to modern warfare or even to war waged between two nuclear powers.

The key question regarding the possible obsolescence of naval power seems to be whether sea power can ever be replaced (or made irrelevant) by air power. This is an old question, asked by visionaries soon after airplanes began regular flights. Importantly, this question has both civil and military implications. The US Army first began making this obsolescence argument in the early 1920s after the July 21, 1921, sinking of a captured German battleship, the *Ostfriesland*, by airplanes. The impact of such demonstrations was not lost on the US Navy; indeed, such demonstrations played a role in fostering naval support for the development of aircraft carrier doctrine in the interwar period. After the atomic bombing of Japan in the Second World War, renewed arguments were made regarding the supposed supremacy of air power.[63] As might be expected, the US Navy was very concerned with this line of strategic argument—and to a lesser extent, even the Army was growing concerned with the claims made be the Air Force. Would future warfare be little more than strategic bombing campaigns carried out by land-based airfleets operating globally?

Douhet's claim that future wars could be won through an application of air power was largely discredited by the experience of World War II and the conflicts that have followed—for example, upon careful examination of German industry following the Second World War, it was learned that the German war industry was not brought to its knees by strategic bombing (though the war industry was of course seriously impacted by the bombing).[64] As Connery explains:

> This much is clear from such studies as have been made: there is no easy way to win a war. Neither high level bombing nor sea blockade won World War II but rather a combination of land and sea and air attacks. In the light of this experience it would be worse than foolhardy to gamble even on atomic bombing as the sole road to victory. Maintaining a balanced striking force made up of components from all three services is far more sound and much better insurance against defeat. Pushbutton wars still remain a thing of the future.[65]

With this analysis of past wars in hand one might expect military practitioners to stop their assault on the value of naval power. It was in large part to demonstrate their service's continued resilience and relevance that the US Navy agreed to the post-war atomic tests at Bikini Atoll. It is true that naval leaders initially were hesitant to acknowledge the severe damage inflicted to the fleet amassed for this exercise.[66] An important lessen was learned: assembling a large fleet, such as the invasion fleet that the United States brought together off of Okinawa in 1944, would merely provide a nuclear armed opponent with a tempting target. Perhaps a target too tempting to pass on even if the conflict had not yet experienced a nuclear exchange. Naval forces would simply have to remain more dispersed than similar task forces in past eras; and no doubt the formation would be much more dispersed than the fleet commander would otherwise desire. This strategic concern for not providing a large target to the enemy translates into a tactical problem for the local fleet commander—but it is a problem that is not insurmountable. Density of the fleet obviously impacts both the offensive and defensive combat strength of the fleet. A more dispersed fleet formation is simply trading on this tactical strength in order to satisfy a new strategic requirement. A dispersed fleet may have difficulty in conducting some naval operations, such as large-scale amphibious landings.[67] Such future landings will no doubt be smaller than the grand invasions of World War II, though their strategic effect may still be quite important.[68]

Despite efforts of naval officials to adapt their doctrine and tactics to the realities of the nuclear era, surprisingly little has changed with regard to criticisms of naval power. Modern criticisms of naval power are evidenced by a current debate the *Naval Institute Proceedings* that was ignited by an article written by a US Air Force officer; this article claims that long-range bombers could perform many of the functions traditionally assigned to surface fleets.[69] Of course this line of argument implies that air power makes not just sea power obsolete, but land power as well.[70] Douhet's ideas retain a powerful hold on many that would see air power ascend to a position of prominence in national military considerations.

## MERCANTILE POWER

Mercantile power, the other side of the sea power coin, has also proven to be a very important component of national power. In recent history, we see that Japan failed as a naval power from 1943–45. In the decades following its military defeat, Japan emerged as a powerful economic power. The initial Japanese post-war economic recover owed much to external influence; in particular, the American change in occupation policy was vital to Japan's recovery. Japanese economic strength became dependent upon international trade to an unprecedented degree. A trading nation that must trade across oceans can not long remain a strong economic power if it fails to remain a strong mercantile power.[71] Without a strong merchant marine a trading nation like Japan becomes dependent upon other nations for its economic existence. Such a high degree of economic dependency becomes a strategic issue, and thus translates directly into political dependency.

Obviously Japan is not the only model of economic success tied in part to sea-borne trading power; South Korea launched its economic advancement in the 1970s with a serious move into the shipbuilding and container carrying industries.[72] Having commodities to trade abroad is obviously an important economic factor; often overlooked is the profitability of shipping the commodities that others produce. Carrying this trade can be highly profitable. Other economic applications of sea power, such as fishing or deep sea oil mining, also present themselves. The Japanese fishing industry is a major part of the Japanese economy; one of the world's largest fishing fleets, it exports some $442.9 billion worth of fish annually as this fleet catches nearly 15 percent of the global catch.[73] In Norway, oil collected in deep-sea oil mining operations represent about 40 percent of Norwegian exports and the economy is highly dependent upon the petroleum industry.

In summation, the following diagram demonstrates the importance of mercantile power to overall economic strength.

**Sources**
Geography
Natural Resources
Capital
Cost of Labor

**Condition**
National dependence on international trade

**Effect**
Successful Shipbuilding
Imports
Exports

## SUMMARY OF THE HISTORY OF SEA POWER

Maritime power has played a decisive role in international relations for centuries. Mahan is well remembered for his attempt to answer a seemingly straightforward question: How has sea power affected world history? Mahan determined that the wealth and power of great empires, particularly of the British Empire, were made possible by the successful use of maritime power. Today nations may not seek empire in the same manner that the British once did; if not hesitant for moral reasons, such empires are now regarded as too expensive and too troublesome politically. Military-political empires may be an ever-more-distant memory, but economic empires are alive and well. Favorable trade and investment arrangements, not colonies, are the stuff of economic power today. Maritime power still enables national economic power and military power projection. Much seems to have changed, but in important way it is only the packaging of the modern international system that is different.

## NOTES

18. See Chapter 1 of Robert Gardiner's *The Earliest Ships*, Naval Institute Press, 1996.

19. Robert Gardiner shows in *The Earliest Ships* that technological advances like the fishing spear and fish hook were not the innovations needed for the development of boats; these innovations only caused the desire to have boats. It was long assumed that early man had simply hallowed out tree trunks when he first attempted to make boats. But these early hunter-gatherers of Central and Western Europe had no tree stock of this size—their available lumber tended to be narrow trunks not suitable for hollowing-out. The technological solution to this problem was another of the Magdalene Culture's new inventions—the sewing needle. As the women of these societies developed their sewing skills, they were able to construct skin boats. Without the newfound ability to make the seams of the boat watertight, the Magdalene boats could not have been developed.

20. "Law of the Sea: The End Game," National Intelligence Council, p. 1.

21. "Law of the Sea: The End Game," National Intelligence Council, p. 1.

22. In *The Earliest Ships* Gardiner traces the use of boats from pure fishing boats, to hunting boats, to boats used for the transportation of goods. It is clear from drawings that have survived the period that ancient man quickly discovered that hunting reindeer (a primary food source) was easily done in rivers as the animal attempted to make a crossing. While swimming, the animal was defenseless, and much slower than even the simple boats in use at the time.

23 It seems that there are always those who would exploit the work of others by stealing what they have. The basic tactic is to lie in wait at some point along the route remote from seaports or coastal towns.

24. Here I use the word "society" loosely to include primitive social organizations led by individual chieftains or oligarchies.

25. The Viking people that terrorized the coasts of Northern Europe are no doubt the best-remembered society that actively supported piracy. However, piracy is not merely a thing of the distant past. *Jane's Intelligence Review* issued a special report on maritime risks and threats in the Western Pacific that docu-

mented the comeback that piracy is making in the Pacific today. An article, "Piracy: Back in Vogue with a Vengeance," *Jane's Intelligence Review*, Special Report No. 7, 1995, explains how relatively weak coast guards have provided modern pirates with ample opportunities to ply their profession in the waters off of Indonesia and the Philippines in the South China Sea (7).

26. See Colonel Trevor Dupuy's *The Evolution of Weapons and Warfare*, Da Capo Paperback, 1984, pp. 8–9. Dupuy points out that merchant boats and ships had been used "for warlike purposes" long before this period, but, it was apparently the Phoenicians who first introduced a vessel designed specifically for war rather than for trade, fishing, or travel.

27. F. E. Adcock, *The Greek and Macedonian Art of War*, University of California Press, 1957, p. 29.

28. See E. B. Potter's *Sea Power: A Naval History*, Naval Institute Press, 1984, for a discussion of this evolution. Modern states have been compelled to defend their maritime interests or suffer the consequences. The US Navy's action against the Barbary pirates in the Mediterranean sent an international message that the United States would not tolerate piracy against American vessels. States unable to send this message can expect their vessels to consistently fall prey to pirates.

29. Bernard Brodie suggests in *Sea Power in the Machine Age*, Princeton University Press, 1941, p. 6, that the history of warfare demonstrates the desire of some to contrive an immediate tactical advantage. Technological innovations are a preferred method of obtaining such advantages. The key has been to satisfy immediate strategic goals before effective counter-measures can be brought to bear by the enemy.

30. As Adcock reminds us in *The Greek and Macedonian Art of War*, p. 29–30, there is no evidence in the *Iliad* that the Trojans had vessels capable of forcing the Achaeans to fight at sea rather than at the gates of Troy.

31. Thucydides makes this claim in Book I of *The Peloponnesian War* (McGraw-Hill, 1982). His often cited analysis of the cause of the war, that "The real cause I consider to be the one which was formally most kept out of sight. The growth of the power of Athens, and the alarm which this inspired in Lacedaemon, made war inevitable" (14), is essentially a consideration of Athenian domination of the Delian League.

32. Alfred Thayer Mahan explains in *The Influence of Sea Power Upon History* (Dover Publications, 1987) that Rome, a traditional land power, was nonetheless able to wrestle command of the sea away from Carthage, a traditional sea power. Roman command of the sea forced Hannibal into his long and dangerous approach to the Italian Peninsula through the Alps, and hindered his re-supply throughout his campaign. Later, the Romans were able to launch a seaborne assault on Carthage in the Third Punic War. The total destruction of Carthage decisively ended the Punic Wars.

33. See Colin Gray's *The Leverage of Sea Power*, The Free Press, 1992.

34. Adcock, *The Greek and Macedonian Art of War*, p. 41.

35. See Crowl's piece in *The Makers of Modern Strategy*, p. 450, Peter Paret editor.

36. Note that relations among states on land are influenced, sometimes decisively, by relations among states at sea.

37. Bernard Brodie, *A Layman's Guide to Naval Strategy*, Princeton University Press, 1942, p 4.

38. The phrase "mercantile power" is used to describe commercial enterprises using the sea as its principal means for moving and/or collecting goods. It is *not* used as a reference to mercantilist economic systems. Mercantile powers recognize that the shipment of commercial goods can be highly profitable. Further, nations that successfully produce commercial (or military) goods may become dependent upon friendly merchant vessels to ship those goods abroad.

39. In "Naval Rivalry," *Jane's Intelligence Review*, Special Report No. 7, 1995, p. 18, it is suggested that the South Korean navy is undergoing a serious naval build-up. By the end of the decade South Korea may have up to 37 modern destroyers and frigates, some 50 corvettes, and numerous fast-attack craft. Recognizing their dependency on friendly naval powers, the South Korean government is attempting to develop independent naval capabilities.

40. Alfred Thayer Mahan, *The Influence of Sea Power Upon History*, 1987 edition, p. 29–58.

41. For example, Geoffrey Till in *Maritime Strategy and the Nuclear Age*, St. Martin's Press, 1984, p. 33.

42. For example, see Crowl's essay in Peter Paret's *The Makers of Modern Strategy from Machiavelli to the Nuclear Age*, Princeton University Press, 1986, p. 447.

43. Much was changing in this era. Steam propulsion was giving vessels greater range and speed. Weapons, from main guns to torpedoes, were increasingly lethal with their payloads deliverable at longer ranges. While naval strategy might survive such changes, naval tactics appeared destined to change.

44. See Crowl in *The Makers of Modern Strategy from Machiavelli to the Nuclear Age*, 1986, p. 447.

45. Midway was not as devastating to the Japanese as Trafalgar was to the French, or Tsushima to the Russians. Nonetheless, Midway represented a significant loss of naval capability—a loss the Japanese lacked the industrial resources to recover during the course of the war. The Battle of Midway did not end serious naval fighting during the Pacific War, but it did mark a decisive turning point during the conflict.

46. The inspiration for this diagram came from Geoffrey Till in *Maritime Strategy and the Nuclear Age*, Second Edition, 1984, p. 13. I have taken the liberty of altering Till's diagram by adding "advanced technologies industries" and "international political system" to the sources column. Note that by adding the "international political system" category, I am significantly altering Till's concept by now adding external variables. I also use a different understanding of "styles of government" since Till was apparently influenced by Alfred Thayer Mahan's "character of the government" when he developed this category. Mahan asserts that different types of political regimes vary in their affinity to sea power (*Influence of Sea Power Upon History: 1660–1783*, p. 58). I disagree. Perceived strategic need, not a particular regime's political philosophy or martial prejudices, guides the desirability of developing maritime power. As a transitory characteristic, I do claim that some governments contain institutionalized bureaucracies that are either more or less receptive to the changes typified and required by modern sea power.

47. The Army Institute for Professional Development considers military strategy to be "the art/science of employing armed forces to secure policy objectives by the use of force or threat of forces. The strategic level of war sets goals and objectives as well as rules of engagement for the military force." Operational art "is the employment of forces to attain strategic goals in a theater of war or operations. Operational art involves decisions about when and where to fight and whether to accept or decline battles." Tactics are said to be "the art by which corps and smaller unit commanders turn potential combat power into victorious battle and engagement." *The Army Institute for Professional Development: Army Correspondence Course Program, Subcourse IT 0469*, "US Army Doctrine, Combat Units, and MI Organizations," p. 2–2.

48. Maneuver "is the movement of forces in relation to the enemy to secure or retain a positional advantage. Effective maneuver keeps the enemy off balance and this helps protect the force. Maneuver occurs at both the operational and the tactical levels." Firepower is defined as "the destructive force essential to defeating the enemy's ability and will to fight. It facilitates maneuver by suppressing the enemy's fires and disrupting the movement of his forces." The third dynamic of combat power, protection, "is the conservation of a fighting force so that it can be effectively used when it is needed. Protection includes those measures taken to prevent the enemy from targeting our troops and equipment, and those actions taken to keep soldiers healthy and high in morale." The last dynamic of combat power, leadership, is valued by the Army as "the most critical element of combat power. It provides purpose, direction, and motivation in combat." *The Army Institute for Professional Development: Army Correspondence Course Program, Subcourse IT 0469*, "US Army Doctrine, Combat Units, and MI Organizations," p. 2–2.

49. Initiative is about "setting or changing the terms of battle by action. It implies an offensive spirit in the conduct of all operations." Note that the "offensive spirit" should be sought even when in a strategic or tactical posture of defense. Agility "is the ability of friendly forces to act faster than the enemy." This speed of thought and action is the first prerequisite for gaining and holding the initiative. Depth refers to "the extension of operations in space, time, and resources. Through the use of depth, a commander obtains the necessary time to plan, arrange, and execute operations, and the necessary resources to win." The last tenet of land warfare is synchronization. Synchronization is "the arrangement of battlefield activities in time, space, and purpose to produce maximum relative combat power at the decisive point. Synchronization is both a process and a result. Commanders synchronize activities; they thereby produce synchronized operations." *The Army Institute for Professional Development: Army Correspondence Course Program, Subcourse IT 0469*, "US Army Doctrine, Combat Units, and MI Organizations," pp. 2–3 through 2–6.

50. See William T. Pendley's "The U.S. Navy, Forward Defense, and the AirLand Battle," pp. 189–199, found in *Emerging Doctrines and Technologies*, Lexington Books, 1988, Pfaltzgraff et al, editors. Pendley offers analysis of the US Army's AirLand Battle doctrine, and discuses its relationship to the US Navy's Maritime Strategy.

51. The US Navy's current confusion, and indeed frustration, concerning the basic tenants of naval warfare is well demonstrated by the constant flood of articles published in *Naval Institute Proceedings* which decry the navy's lack of strategic doctrine. See Lieutenant William J. Roger's "Toward a Doctrine of U.S. Naval Power," December 1996, Rear Admiral Joseph F. Callo's "Finding Doctrine's Future In the Past," October 1996, Ensign Patrick M. Kelly's "The U.S. Navy Must Re-Evaluate Its Doctrine," July 1996, James J. Tritten's "Maneuver Warfare at Sea," September 1995, or Lieutenant Jeffrey R. Macris' "Is Mahan Relevant?," May 1995.

52. The American example is not unique. As the British Royal Navy forged the British Empire rigid operational orders rather than true doctrine guided the fleet. Such rigidity was influential in the French victory over the British at Chesapeake Bay during the American War for Independence.

53. William T. Pendley, "The U.S. Navy, Forward Defense, and the AirLand Battle," pp. 189–199, found in *Emerging Doctrines and Technologies*, 1988, Pfaltzgraff et al, editors.

54. Mahan argues that past naval strategies serve to illustrate "principles" of naval warfare that are timeless. While he acknowledges that a great deal of change regularly occurs in the area of tactics (for Mahan tactics begin at the point were opposing "fleets come into collision at the point to which strategic consid-

erations have brought them" p. 9), he claims that "the teachings of history have a more evident and permanent value, because the conditions remain more permanent." Found in *The Influence of Sea Power Upon History*, pp. 7–9. Crowl has a good treatment of Mahan's problems in formulating principles of sea power in Peter Paret's *Makers of Modern Strategy from Machiavelli to the Nuclear Age*.

55. The US Navy publication ". . . From the Sea" has the phrase "Preparing the Naval Service for the 21st Century" prominently listed on its cover.

56. Till, Ibid., p. 15. The titles, "means, effect and ends" are my own, not Till's.

57. The point of decisive battle, or rather the point of strategy, is to force the enemy to engage in battles whose loss will be decisive—that is, it will determine the outcome of campaigns and wars. If the United States had been defeated at Midway, the outcome would not have been decisive for the Japanese conduct of the war. The United States could recover its losses, even retake Hawaii if it came to that, and continue to carry out its basic national strategy. The Japanese could not expect to invade and conquer the United States in order to end the war favorably. But, the United States could continue to build toward the invasion of Japan.

58. The example of the combined French–Spanish Fleet being more useful as a fleet-in-being is an obvious example. Even single warships have been useful in this role. The Royal Navy's fear of the *Bismarck* was out of all proportion to the effectiveness of that great warship. Perhaps the Germans would have been better off by keeping her threat implied, instead of active.

59. For more reading of the value of navies in the atomic era please see Vice-Admiral Sir Peter Gretton in *Maritime Strategy: A Study of Defense* Problems, , or Colin Gray in *The Leverage of Sea Power*, 1992. These writers argue convincingly that naval power has not lost its utility in the nuclear age.

60. By "hard-target" I here refer to those military targets that are immobile and known to the enemy. In this sense, both Ft. Bragg and Washington DC are military targets whose location is known. An army in the field is not a hard target, since it is mobile. However, no army has yet achieved the mobility of a naval fleet. While fleets at sea are easier to detect than they once were, their opportunity for stealth still surpasses that of land forces.

61. The *Military Balance* has current listings of weapons systems aboard principal combatants. Also see *Jane's Ships and Aircraft of the US Navy* or *Combat Fleets of the World* for further descriptions of modern weapons systems and their capabilities.

62. The US Congress issued a report on the Bikini Atoll test that is well worth reading: "Radiation Exposure from the Pacific Nuclear Tests," Committee of Natural Resources. The test was code named Operation Crossroads by the United States. The May/June 1993 issue of *American History Illustrated* has an

excellent article on the operation, "Operation Crossroads," for those who wish to understand the military backdrop of the tests. David Bradley's *No Place to Hide*, University Press of New England, 1983 edition, is a good place to start for those wishing to examine this series of tests against the growing moral dilemma that atomic weapons were causing in the west. The US government's official position on the tests and impressive pictures of the tests are shown in the Office of the Historian, Joint Task Force One's *Operation Crossroads: The Official Pictorial Record*, Wm. H. Wise & Co., Inc., 1946.

63. Guidio Douhet wrote *Domin io dell' aria (Command of the Air)* in 1921 (see the Coward McCann Inc., edition, 1942). Bernard Brodie's *Strategy in the Missile Age*, Princeton University Press, 1959, shows how one could theoretically bypass an adversary's traditional military power altogether. The thought of bypassing an enemy's strength, say his army, and directly attacking him at his political or economic center sounds too good to be true, and probably is. A competent enemy will either develop similar offensive capabilities (which make your capability of dubious advantage since he can hurt you in the same manner), develop defensive capabilities (which negate your original advantage), or some combination of both.

64. The point is not that air power did not have an impact; rather, the point is that it is difficult to determine opportunity cost comparisons in a "what if" situation. The 1,000 aircraft bombing raids to Germany damaged communications, transportation, industrial production, fuel production, and electrical production. Not the least of the effect was to force Germany to build interceptor aircraft to shoot down allied bombers, rather than building bombers to attack strategic targets or support German ground forces. Some 850,000 men were tied up in the German ground-based air-defenses. Thousands of anti-aircraft guns that could have been used to destroy Russian, American, and British tanks were employed to shoot down airplanes over the Third Reich. All of the materials that went into air defense—telephones, searchlights, wire and cable, motor transport—could have been used by German field armies to destroy allied armies on the ground. Had the allies not bombed Germany, German industry would have operated at full strength and the German war effort would not have needed to concentrate on tools to stop the bombing. Of course, allied forces would also have been concentrating on the land battle had they neglected air assaults—perhaps the end result would have been the same. Speculation aside, we know that it took competent, and fairly large armies to beat the Germans; control of the air and sea were not enough.

65. Robert H. Connery, *The Navy and the Industrial Mobilization in World War II*, Da Capo Press, 1972, p. 447. This is not to say that Connery's opinion is uncontroversial. It must be considered that the scale of strategic bombing undertaken in 1944 had not been applied in 1941 and 1942. It was not then possible be-

cause US heavy bombers did not begin bombing Germany from England unit August 17, 1942—then with 12 B17s of the 97th Bomb Group stationed at Roven-Sotterville. It is not until January 27, 1943, that the US Eighth Air Force in England bombs Germany—then with 53 heavy bombers hitting Wilkelmshaven and Emden. This lack of initial bombing is due to the drain on American resources early in a global war. The US support of the Twelve Air Force in North Africa necessarily drained support from units operating in England; this, of course, says nothing of the drain from the war in the Pacific. Further, initial bombing missions out of England targeted German submarine pens in France at Brent, St. Nogaire, and L'Oreint. It is not until March 18, 1943, that the Eighth Air Force marshaled almost 100 aircraft (97) to attack submarine yards in Germany. On May 18, 1943, the Royal Air Force and Eighth Air Force institute the well-known policy of RAF night bombing and American day bombing. On June 22, a 182 heavy bomber mission over the Ruhr is tried—there is still a drain in resources from the Mediterranean theater. It is not until August 15, 1943, that Eighth Air Force can marshal over 300 heavy bombers for one mission. On February 20, 1944, the Eighth Air Force (for the first time) puts over 1,000 heavy bombers into the air over Germany. The British were able to reach such numbers a few months earlier in raids over Berlin. Thus, some argue that upon a close investigation of the facts we find that allied forces were not engaging in an effective air campaign until quite late in the war. Sir Charles Webster and A. Noble Franksland's *History of the Second World War, United Strategic Bombing Survey (USGPO)*, and *The Strategic Air Offensive*, H. M. Stationary Office, 1961.

66. See David Bradley's *No Place to Hide.*

67. Theodore L. Gatchel offers an excellent analysis of past amphibious landings in *At the Water's Edge: Defending against the Modern Amphibious Assault*, Naval Institute Press, 1996. The author stresses lessons learned from past operations (from Gallipoli to the Falkland Islands) and suggests, counter-intuitively, that amphibious operations tend to be successful, if costly.

68. Remember that the Army and Marine Corps exist in an era of declining force structures. Even a modest amphibious task force today would pack quite a punch once on land. An Army 2x2 brigade is a much more formidable and independent force than it was in World War II. While landings on the scale of the Normandy landings may never occur again, perhaps such landing are no longer needed.

69. Captain James W. Fryer, "Flying With the Bone." *Naval Institute Proceedings*, February 1995, p. 49. Captain Fryer argues for joint Air Force-Navy power projection operations. In and of itself this argument appears quite sensible; but it is based upon the assumption that land-based aircraft can complement (or in some cases replace) carrier-based aircraft. This article touched off a series of let-

ters to the editor and articles making counter claims. The November 1996 edition was still receiving letters and articles referencing this very sensitive naval issue.

70. The US Air Force published a report, "Reaching Globally, Reaching Powerfully: The United States Air Force in the Gulf War," (September 1991) which asserted that the Air Force was the decisive arm in the Gulf War. Rather than merely "preparing" the battlefield for the US Army, this report proudly claims that air power had "destroyed" the battlefield well before ground forces began their assault.

71. Obviously it is possible to have one's goods carried on the vessels of other nations. This can work well so long as access to foreign vessels exists. However, this practice leaves the nation dependent upon the goodwill of others— never a sound strategic practice.

72. In *Asia's Next Giant: South Korea and Late Industrialization*, Oxford University Press, 1989, pp. 269–290, Alice H. Amsden shows how Hyundai Heavy Industries (HHI), a subsidiary of the Hyundai Group, built its first ship in 1973. Within a decade, HHI became the world's largest shipbuilder; South Korea's overall share of world orders for new ships reached 18.9 percent in 1986. In part to provide HHI with a committed customer, the Hyundai Group founded a general trading company: the Hyundai Merchant Marine Company. South Korea's move into shipbuilding and commodity trading has proven very profitable, and has helped to spur general South Korean industrialization.

73. *World Factbook*, 1995, pp. 215–17 and *The Information Please Almanac: 1997*, p. 213.

# CHAPTER 2

# The Impact of Technological Innovation

*We live in an unusual world, marked by very
great and irreversible changes that occur within
the span of a man's life. We live in a time where
our knowledge and understanding of the world
of nature grows wider and deeper at an unparalleled rate; and where the problems of applying this knowledge to man's needs and hopes
are new, and only a little illuminated by our
past history.*

—J. ROBERT OPPENHEIMER, *UNCOMMON SENSE*


*A nation which invests a great deal of money
and uses its best minds in industries directly
oriented toward war production will eventually
possess arms as good or better than those of a
rival whose industry has nonetheless a superior
average productivity.*

—RAYMOND ARON, *PEACE AND WAR*


## SCIENCE, TECHNOLOGY, AND HUMAN PROGRESS

We live in an era of great scientific and technological discovery. Innovative uses of existing scientific and technological knowledge are merged
with new discoveries; many significant scientific and technological innovations will be observed during the lifetime of someone born today. It is
impossible to fully understand how fundamentally these future advances
will impact the everyday lives of people. If the twentieth century is used
as a guide for the life-changing innovations that the twenty-first century
may bring, then the possibilities seem only limited by human imagination. Men would engage in powered and controlled flight at the beginning of the century; a mere 44 years later the speed of sound would be

met and passed in an aircraft—an aircraft as distant from the one used in 1903 at Kitty Hawk as today's personal computers are distant from the abacus. The power of the atom would be unleashed in wartime, and harnessed for humanitarian purposes in peacetime. Men would walk on the moon and send probes to explore distant galaxies. Few have observed the growth of computer technology over the last twenty years, made obvious to all of us with the success of the PC for home use, without developing a sense of scientific and technical ascendancy in modern society. Looking at all of this change in the span of a single lifetime calls into question whether this degree of change has always occurred so quickly in human history, or whether something new is afoot. Oppenheimer's quote suggests that engineers and physical scientists have formed a consensus that mankind's accumulated knowledge is growing at ever faster rates.[74] This implies that the next century will be even more dynamic than the amazing twentieth century in terms of scientific and technological discovery.

How can we know, much less prove, that mankind's accumulated knowledge is growing at faster rates than in past periods of history?[75] That accumulated knowledge is growing is clear; the rate of its growth can only be determined if an effective measurement of knowledge is available. In truth it is difficult to create a good standard for the measurement of something as intangible and abstract as "mankind's accumulated knowledge." To start, where shall the line be drawn between new discoveries and mere technological improvement? How shall the relative value of a new invention or innovation be weighed? These difficulties aside, of course some still make the attempt to take such measurements. For example, there are those who suggest that counting the number of scientific patents awarded in successive years—and thus discovering that these patents are increasing annually as a historic trend—is one manner of demonstrating that mankind is developing knowledge at ever faster rates. Another method for demonstrating the increasing rate of scientific and technological discovery has been the measurement of journal articles in scientific and technological periodicals. As with the number of patents, it has been demonstrated that the volume of journal articles in growing exponentially. Though both of these techniques are highly convenient measurement tools, since the data needing to be counted is readily available, such measurements are problematic in that they must assume that one patent or article is as important as the next. In effect all of these measurements incorporate a fallacious system of counting. Although these measurements support my contention that technological innovation has come to experience exponential growth, I am forced to reject the inherent assumptions in these proofs. A patent for a new medicine in the treatment of cancer is not to be confused with a patent for new style of tongue depressor. Thus, we are left with a commonly held supposition that really cannot be proven, a conviction held by professionals and laymen alike that things are progressing faster than ever before. For the sake of this paper I accept the hypothesis that mankind's accumulated scientific and technological knowledge is in fact growing exponentially rather than in a linear fashion. It is not in doubt that the rate of technological discovery increased through recent centuries. The unknown is whether it will continue to increase at the same exponential rate in the future. It is easy to be satisfied with the safe assumption that it will continue to develop (and perhaps rapidly), but hesitate to consider the implications of a continued exponential growth. My research and observations suggest a continuation to the phenomena of exponential growth; I thus chose to consider that which appears likely rather than the assumption that is safe. I admit to having no solid proof that this phenomena is in fact occurring, and I fully understand that the appearance of a quickening rate of scientific and technical innovation may be an illusion.[76] Still, for the moment, let us take a small leap and assume that our cumulative gut feeling is in fact correct. What then are the geopolitical implications of this trend?

## THE MEANING OF SCIENCE AND TECHNOLOGY

Science and technology are essentially two sides of the same coin; the technological innovation that this paper concerns itself with is predicated on scientific innovation. In *Science and Human Values* Bronowski defines science in the following way:

> My purpose is to talk about science as it is, practical and theoretical. I define science as the organization of our knowledge in such a way that it commands more of the hidden potential of nature. What I have in mind therefore is both deep and matter of fact; it reaches from the kinetic theory of gases to the telephone and the suspension bridge and medicated toothpaste. It admits no sharp boundary between knowledge and use. There are of course people who like to draw a line between pure and applied science; and oddly, they are often the same people who find art unreal. . . .[77]

According to Bronowski, then, science and technology are part of the same process; boundaries between scientific "knowledge" and technological "use" are in most ways artificial. Despite the conventional understanding of science and technology as different sides of the same coin, I have chosen to emphasize technology in this paper, or what Bronowski calls "applied science," because in military affairs an innovation on the drawing board pales when compared to an innovation in actual use on the battlefield. Indeed, the time taken to turn a theoretical breakthrough into a practical new weapon system is critical in the real world. Thus, for our purposes speaking of scientific innovations is usually not specific enough; we must instead be sure that all understand we are speaking of the final step in the process: technological innovation.

## PACE OF INNOVATION

Technological innovation is an important component of military success. Some of the losing nations in the age of empire, like India and China, were nations with long and proud martial traditions. Despite their traditions these societies could not overcome the technological advantages of their opponents.[78] Near the end of the eighteenth century Britain was the first nation to begin industrialization. Holding and expanding the British Empire was predicated on superior industrial prowess. Obviously the British were not the first people to take advantage of superior technology in military applications; nor would they be the last. As the "Second Industrial Revolution" occurred toward the end of the nineteenth century, the relative technological advantage gained by Germany and the United States near the end of the nineteenth century would propel these nations onto the world stage as successful industrial and military powers.[79]

Historically the pace of mankind's industrial development and advancement has been relatively slow; that is, major states have had the opportunity to catch up with their competitors by observing the function of new developments and copying them. Though specific technological expertise might have varied from field to field, the overall effect throughout much of recorded history was a more or less technologically level playing field among major states. Starting in the late 1700s a change began to occur; some nations (led by Britain) were clearly establishing lasting relative technological leads. Although some change in rankings of relative technological proficiency has occurred, as a rule we discover that in the late twentieth century the relative technological leads that began centuries ago remain quite large. The types of technology that began to be adapted in the 1700s were different from earlier innovations; more precisely, these were advances that begin to feed directly and promptly into future innovations. The British were the first to achieve a sort of critical mass of technological innovation that began to feed on itself. Other nations had difficulty closing the gap with the British because the development of an industrial base from which to compete technologically is difficult. The Germans and Americans were able to compete with the British only after each made a tremendous investment in industrial infrastructure.

Today the pace of technological advance is quickening among those nations that posses the industrial base from which to compete in the field of advanced technology. This phenomena, as opposed to individual technological advances, is now the most significant factor in the development of military power. The US Marine Corps Commandant, General Krulak, recently stated that "Rapid advances in science and technology are bringing vastly increased lethality to conventional weapons, and are making weapons of mass destruction more available."[80] Though still concerned about specific weapons systems, General Krulak is apparently becoming interested in the speed of technological advances. The rate of technological innovation already has had a tremendous impact on naval power.

The strategic importance of high technology has now achieved widespread public awareness in industrialized nations. In addition to the lessons that CNN taught all of us during the Gulf War, consider literature like the book *The Japan That Can Say No*. In this 1991 book Shintaro Ishihara suggests that the United States is totally dependent upon Japanese computer chips—militarily as well as economically. This book was highly popular in Japan in the mid 1980s, as it claimed that Japan could at will render America a muscle-bound invalid. In the United States similar arguments concerning dependence upon technology have been made. Toffler and Toffler's vision of the Third Wave of warfare in *War and Anti-war* has become widely assimilated in the population at large. The Tofflers and other writers deal with the concept of information warfare; pundits have claimed that information warfare represents a paradigm change in modern warfare.[81] To demonstrate the possibilities found with information warfare the Tofflers offer the following example.

> On January 19, 1991, in the allied air attack on Baghdad, the U.S. Navy used Tomahawk cruise missiles to deliver what *Defense News* described as "a new class of highly secret, non-nuclear electromagnetic pulse warheads" to disrupt or destroy Iraqi electronic systems. Such weapons cause no overt physical damage but can 'fry' the components of radar, electronic networks, and computers.[82]

Such "information" weapons sound too good to be true in part because the Gulf War may be an unusual example. In the Gulf high-tech allied military forces fought strictly conventional Iraqi forces. The US led coalition might not have faired as well against a more technically competent nation. Some suggest that "this information advantage can help deter or defeat traditional military threats at relatively low cost," while others temper such talk with the reminder that "the simple and brutal fact remains that force works by destroying and killing . . . And fear of violent death only comes from the imminent possibility of the real thing."[83]

## SCIENCE, TECHNOLOGY, AND MILITARY POWER

Technological advances have transformed life in industrialized nations. As Brodie points out in *Sea Power in the Machine Age*, technology's affect on man's nature may be minimal—our culture and basic mores may remain fundamentally unchanged by advances in technology. Thus, the foundations of decisions regarding which national policies and security requirements are worth engaging in warfare over may be little changed; technology, of itself, does not seem ready to change why or when military force is utilized. Nonetheless, technology's affect on the conduct of man's quarrels has been dramatic.[84] The impact of new technologies on warfare has been a topic of great interest to both scholars and military professionals for centuries.[85] In *Ballistics in the Seventeenth Century*, Hall claims

> The relations of science and the art of war are similar to those of science and technology. Indeed, from the point of view of statesmen they are identical, for the power and skill of the state in making war depend (among other things) upon its technological development, and this in turn depends upon the application of science. This truth had been dimly apprehended in the late sixteenth century, and in the age of Newton was too clear to require demonstration. It was apparent to Colbert when he founded the Academie Royale des Sciences and it was urged by Leibniz as a reason for founding a similar scientific assembly in Germany.[86]

Why then does a myth of military resistance to new technology and invention exist in the public mind? Military leaders tend to be conservative in nature; and it is true that military organizations once resisted the introduction of untested (and thus to the military mind untrustworthy) new weapons. Better to trust the weapon of proven value than the drawing board potential of something new. Hall observes that the desire for advanced weaponry is not always found in government and military officials. There are periods where governments may have little desire to fund new arms expenditures, and where military leaders may be "tolerably well satisfied" with the weapons they already posses. It is with such observations that clichés are born stating that 'the generals are always preparing to win the last war.' Of course military leaders are acutely interested in those weapons, doctrine, and tactics that seemed successful in recent combat operations—should they ignore such success? Any resistance to new weapons, doctrine, or tactics is rooted in an unwillingness to take chances on the unproved. Far from being foolishly unimaginative regarding innovative forms of warfare, military leaders hesitate to gamble on the untested with the security of their nation. But, something has changed. The military leader's commitment to assuring the security of his nation now leads him to embrace innovations in weapons, and even to embrace innovations in doctrine and tactics, since there may no longer be time to meaningfully adapt to such innovations during the course of a war.

We must hesitate to make any assumption that future warfare will necessarily be decided in a short time frame. History teaches us that "short war" theories have been mistakenly assumed in past eras; the most notable example is found in predictions about the likely duration of a general war in Europe on the eve of World War I.[87] Why should today's predictions, couched in language like 'modern warfare is a come as you are affair,' be any more accurate? In fact, in a war fought by two evenly matched combatants, there is still little reason to assume a short conventional war. For example, had the Cold War turned hot it is entirely conceivable that the combat would have lasted years; this is particularly likely if nuclear weapon use was restricted. The modern change to the expected duration of combat operations is found in the nature of the "even matching" of military capabilities of the combatants. Rough parity in military capabilities has never been easier to lose in a short period of time. The speed with which military equipment (and accompanying doctrine) becomes obsolete is unprecedented in history. The fear of following behind, then, is behind the military establishment's modern commitment to technological innovation.

Today's generals and admirals speak of a technological paradigm shift—a new era of flux wherein new weapons guide operational art to an unprecedented degree. During the Cold War the Russians became convinced that this shift represented a fundamental transformation in the nature of warfare; a shift they referred to as a "military-technical revolution."[88] The irony of this Russian strategic insight is that the Soviet Union lacked the scientific and technological expertise required to bring this revolution to the

Soviet armed forces. Following the dramatic American victory in the Gulf
War, Secretary of Defense Richard Cheney spoke of the war as demonstrating the possibilities of the military-technological revolution.[89] Conventional
strategic conceptions that tended to minimize the positive impact of new
technologies on the battlefield were being turned on their head. Gray ex-
presses the traditional view of academics and military professionals who
study the impact of technology on warfare when he wrote

> The key to temporary success in war tends to lie in the novel use of
> new, or newly combined, weapons rather than in those weapons them-
> selves. No major war between industrial powers has been won because
> one side was technologically superior. The case of Japan in 1945 is not
> really an exception, given the many areas in which Japanese deficien-
> cies were literally critical. Weapons do not win or lose wars, either for
> states that enjoy a comparable level of technological achievement, or
> even for states with different levels of technological achievement,
> when the parameters of the conflict (such as triple-cover jungle) place
> brute force at a large discount.[90]

Such sentiments are consistent, for example, with Jomini's dictum that
changing weaponry affects the practice of warfare, but not the principles
of warfare.[91] For example, it is often pointed out that the successful German use of *Blitzkrieg* tactics early in World War II built upon a new doctrinal use of weapons, notably the tank and aircraft, that had both first
seen combat in World War I. Thus it is suggested that it was "the novel
use" of armor formations and divebombers, and not new armored technology or aircraft engineering, that made the difference for German arms
early in World War II. Put another way, these weapons were first used in-
correctly (or at least ineffectively). Numerous examples of decisive victories resulting from innovative uses of existing weapons, rather than
from new weapons, can be found throughout history. Those skeptical of
new technology immediately translating into military advantage are
quick to point out that the aircraft, the submarine, and the machine-gun
all took years to become meaningfully deployed.[92] The creative use of
existing weapons no doubt is very important; as are, also no doubt, creative improvements to those existing weapons and the doctrines that
guide their use. Still, those who downplay the impact of new technology
on the battlefield, however, often miss two important points. First, there
have been new technologies that have led to new weapons that in turn
have had an immediate impact on the battlefield. Second, even with those

technologies (or actual weapons systems) that were not fully appreciated early in their life cycles, we find that the time lag from initial development to meaningful deployment is growing ever shorter.

As to the first point, the Italian development of large, long-range, strategic bombers in World War I made it possible to operate raids on Austrian targets with as many as 250 bombers at a time.[93] Those who would point to the British and American bombing campaigns of World War II as the first doctrinally sensible use of aircraft in warfare have neglected an important precedent set by the Italians. Allied development of the tank, a new weapon in the First World War, made an immediate impact in the war by breaking the stalemate on the Western Front. Despite the conventional analysis, a careful examination shows that the tank did not wait until World War II to have a significant impact in combat operations.[94] In "New Ways of War" Rosen demonstrates successful military innovations in Britain (radar) and the United States (aircraft carriers and amphibious assaults).[95] The British experience with radar is particularly illuminating. During World War I Britain suffered from German air raids.[96] In the interwar period the British military concluded that such raids would become increasingly devastating as aircraft technology improved.[97] To maximize the effectiveness of defensive intercept aircraft, the key would be to improve available information about the incoming enemy air attack. Thus, when radar was successfully demonstrated to the British military, still on an experimental basis in 1935, it met with an already appreciated doctrinal need. Incredibly, by the end of 1936 the RAF was already operating training facilities for radar operators.[98] As Rosen summaries, "An understanding of the requirement for air defense intelligence thus existed before radar. When improved intelligence became a technological possibility, its importance was quickly understood."[99] The Germans would also develop radar during the war, but they would lag slightly behind British science in their radar's capabilities, and would lag significantly behind the British military in the doctrinal use of the radar. Lacking a well-defined mission for the new technology, the German experience with radar was less successful. Almost simultaneously the United States was also developing radar, though it was hoped that it would serve a very different military requirement. The US Army had the responsibility of defending the American coastline from enemy landings. In support of this mission, the Coast Artillery submitted a requirement to the Army Signal Corps for the development of a means of observing at long range ships and aircraft that were approaching the United States. Under-funded and under-staffed during the late 1920s and early 1930s, the Signal Corps nonetheless successfully tested radar in 1935. The US Navy quickly became interested in the Army's development; as America entered World War II US warships were already being equipped with radar sets. Again we find a doctrinal need filled quickly with emerging technological capabilities. The Allied experience with radar is not unique. High-frequency direction finders (HF/DF) were thought by the Germans to be mostly an experimental technology in naval warfare. Even if operational on the largest classes of vessels, German experts mistakenly assumed that HF/DF could not be used on small escort warships, like destroyers and corvettes, because of their space requirements and weight. Unknown to the Germans was the fact that the Allies had successfully, and secretly, miniaturized the components of HF/DF. This successful application of a new technology to actual combat use at sea played a significant role in the Battle of the Atlantic.[100] Obviously there are historic examples of a new technology not being appreciated early in its life cycle. This should not surprise anyone. Yet, if even some important technologies have been applied initially in a sensible manner, this suggests that it may happen again. To be sure, there is no guarantee that a given nation will comprehend the military significance of modern scientific and engineering discoveries; the point is, the nation may understand.

Obviously victors are not the only nations capable of innovation. In World War II the Germans were able to successfully develop and deploy their V weapons. In *Crusade in Europe*, Eisenhower claimed that had the Germans perfected their V weapons six months earlier, the D-day landings might not have been possible. Certainly Eisenhower was in an excellent position to know the veracity of this claim.[101] Of course many will say that while "could have beens" are fascinating to discuss, Germany ultimately lost the war even with its new rockets. The German investment in "super-weapons" that might turn the course of the war ultimately produced too little too late; such programs should have been started much earlier in the war to be given a chance.[102] Though not ultimately decisive in that conflict, the new rocket development had great potential, aided the German war cause, and the rockets were deployed appropriately from the beginning. The fact that the German rocket program had truly great potential is evident in the well-known Russian vs. American/British rush to capture German rocket scientists and technicians in the closing days of the conflict. Little can speak so clearly to the real effect of German rocket warfare as the Allies desire to have those weapons for themselves. As a historic trend, the deployment of new technologies has become both faster and more suitable to the technologies potential than at any time in history. As we see with the German example in World War II, new technologically advanced weapons do not guarantee victory, though they can extend a conflict and make final victory more costly for an adversary.

For an example of a truly decisive introduction of a new weapon, note that it took less than a month from the first successful American test detonation of an atomic bomb to its actual use in combat.[103] For both the eventual winners and losers of wars, we observe that new technology can lead to advanced weapons that are properly and decisively utilized early in their life cycle. Of course, new technologies need not be incorporated into a new weapon system *per se* to have a significant military impact. As Dandeker points out in *The Bureaucratization of Force*, in the nineteenth century railways provided the technological tool for solving the equation between military power and the size of the available adult male population.[104] Might an advance in something like artificial computer intelligence today bridge the gap between military power and declining force structures? It is important to emphasize that the innovation itself need not be in an area we would normally consider "military;" all that is required of the innovation is that some bright person envision an effective military usage.

As to the second issue, that even with those technologies (or actual weapons systems) that were not correctly utilized early in their life cycles, the time lag from initial development to appropriate deployment is growing ever shorter. In the nineteenth century it took better than fifty years for the British Navy to make the complete conversion from sail to steam power after the invention of the first steam-powered ship in 1802; this contrasts sharply against the early twentieth century when it took less than fifteen years for the British to adopt military air power after the 1903 heavier-than-air demonstration at Kitty Hawk.[105] Obviously military professionals will never achieve a perfect record of matching a new development's potential with its initial tactical deployment—this is asking for too much. Just as automotive engineers may be slow to appreciate the relevance of safety features to their profession, so too may men and women in uniform make the occasional misjudgment. While one navy may, for example, misread the importance of a new system of underwater propulsion, a second navy may grasp its potential from the start. The key may lie in the development of military organizations that are aggressive in their application of emerging technologies to their profession. It is noteworthy that military professionals increasingly are schooled in cutting edge technologies themselves, and that their initial deployment of new technologies is both faster and more appropriate than at any time in history.[106] The level of institutional complacency (ironically caused in part by past success) may emerge as a useful gauge of organizational responsiveness to new technological developments.

A consideration of technological advances in military equipment may, to some, be interesting of itself. Students of international politics must strive to infer the deeper international implications, military and political, of such technological innovations. Brodie suggests that there are three issues relevant questions to consider.

> What changes in the tactics of war are brought about in each instance? What is the significance of the development in the larger field of strategy? How do these changes in tactics and strategy, possibly coupled with other and more direct influences, affect the power balance between individual states?[107]

Brodie's questions remain appropriate. Importantly, these questions are prioritized from least important to most important. Tactical changes, if significant, may compel changes in basic strategy. Nations that fail to adapt to new strategic demands may suffer severe consequences. Most important is the manner in which various changes in tactics or strategy effect the international balance of power.

## THE MYTH OF THE BATTLESHIP ADMIRALS

To date, the rate of technological advance has been neglected in security studies. Conventional wisdom asserts that it takes many years, perhaps decades, for military organizations to successfully incorporate new technologies into decisive weapons. If true, any quickening in the rate of technological innovation would be diluted by the slow application of that technology. Perhaps the most lasting image of a military organization resisting technological innovation is found with the interwar western navies, particularly the US Navy's, reluctance to adapt their fleets to the emerging demands of naval air power. In fact, this myth of the "Battleship Admirals" resisting change is grossly incorrect. In dismissing conventional arguments that nations were slow to adapt new technologies, such as the aircraft, to military uses, Terraine offers the following observation

> The outstanding feature of the story of aviation is the speed of its development. The maritime role of aircraft tells the same tale: only six years elapsed between the Wright brothers' breakthrough at Kitty Hawk in 1903 and Bleriot's Channel crossing in 1909 which first made light of

the sea. Thereafter, the air assault on the water barrier, which throughout human history had been the chief constraint upon the movement of man, progressed by rapid strides. The year after Bleriot's flight saw the first step taken towards a sea-carrier for aircraft, when Eugene Ely took off from the deck of an American cruiser; the next year (1911) he capped that by landing on USS Pennsylvania and then taking off again.[108]

Whether it is advanced steel processing, new optical devices, or new power plants, nations are normally committed to putting their best technological effort forward when it comes to sea power. Let us examine the American interwar experience with naval air power in more detail.

Many people are familiar with the July 21, 1921, sinking of a captured German battleship by airplanes during a test conducted by the US Navy and US Army. Most recall only that the ship was sunk and that the Navy's hierarchy was upset with Army General Billy Mitchell's conduct during the test. Mitchell's sinking of the *Ostfriesland* is remembered as a highly controversial test of air power. The US Navy claimed that Mitchell's Army aviators had broken the rules governing the test, but to most people such technicalities did nothing to dispute the fact that the ship was sunk. In fact, such "rules" have a reasonable place in wargames. The *Ostfriesland*, for the obvious reason that it was a target ship, was not manned during the test. The Navy claimed that a manned warship would be both maneuvering and engaging the attacking aircraft in a real engagement.[109] Many of the "rules" put into effect during this test were in fact efforts to simulate problems attacking aircraft would realistically experience; Mitchell's flying low and slow over a stationary target was, to be fair to the Navy, not a reasonable test of aircraft capabilities. Lost in history is the fact that the Navy had *earlier* conducted its own independent test of the effect of air power on surface combatants in November 1920. An old battleship, the USS *Indiana*, was used as the target ship in this forgotten test. Mitchell (a proponent of Army air power) had discovered that the secret test had occurred and had obtained pictures of the battle damage to the *Indiana*, and leaked those pictures to the press.[110] Public pressure led the Navy to conduct the more public test with the *Ostfriesland*, with Mitchell's Army aviators participating.

While the US Navy was developing an understanding of the defensive requirements the fleet would need if subjected to air attack, they did not neglect the potential to deliver an air attack upon an enemy fleet. At the close of the First World War, the British Navy had five aircraft carriers in service, the HMS *Argus, Eagle, Furious, Hermes,* and *Vindictive*.[111] Large carriers were not the only British carrier innovation during World

War I.[112] American naval officers served during the war with their British counterparts and observed firsthand the direction being taken by the most capable navy in the world.[113] There is ample evidence of serious and professional discussion in American naval circles concerning international naval developments during this period. Though behind the British in the development of carriers, the US Navy had not been neglecting air power prior to World War I. As early as 1898, Assistant Secretary of the Navy Theodore Roosevelt had expressed interest in the military value of Professor Langley's flying machine.[114] Roosevelt recommended the formation of an inter-service board to evaluate the effectiveness of this still mostly theoretical machine; the board reported favorably on experimentation in the use of aircraft as military weapons. On the eve of World War I the US Navy issued a news release stating

> The Secretary of the Navy has decided that the science of aerial navigation has reached that point where aircraft must form a large part of our naval force for offensive and defensive operations. Nearly all countries having a Navy are giving attention to this subject. This country has not fully recognized the value of aeronautics in preparation for war, but it is believed we should take our proper place.[115]

Despite evidence suggesting an early, and official, American interest in naval aviation, the myth of official indifference continues.

During the interwar period two potential naval threats were seen by American admirals—the Japanese Navy and the British Navy—for the sensible reason that these navies were the only forces deemed capable of challenging the US Fleet.[116] American admirals did not miss the significant British and Japanese developments in naval air warfare.[117] Historical evidence clearly shows that the American "Battleship Admirals" had not been remiss in their professional obligations.[118] In 1921 the United States completed the conversion of a fleet collier[119] into an aircraft carrier, the USS *Langley*. Although the United States was a few years behind the British[120], the conversion of this first American carrier was actually completed before the first two Japanese carriers, the *Kaga* and *Hosho*, became operational in November 1921.[121] The *Langley* was intended to give the navy practical experience in naval air operations. Lessons learned in operations with the *Langley* were incorporated into the USS *Lexington* and *Saratoga*, both completed in 1925 (and both commissioned in 1927). For example, modifications were made to the design of later vessels to enable aircraft to land more safely in any weather.[122] The 1920s also found David S. Ingalls become the Assistant Secretary of the Navy (Air). Ingalls had been a naval aviator in France during World War I; he was the US Navy's first ace and had received the Distinguished Service Medal.[123] His appointment suggests that not only was the Navy Department serious enough about air warfare to adapt their highest levels of organization to reflect the new weapon platform, but it even went so far as to place an individual serious about air warfare into such a high profile position. Under Ingalls' leadership (during the Hoover administration) significant research and development was conducted in naval air warfare. He would return to active duty in World War II, eventually retiring as a rear admiral in the Naval Reserve.

The acquisition of aircraft carriers suggests that the US Navy envisioned a role for that class of vessel in future warfare; the characteristics of that role would soon come into focus in a series of innovative wargames. During war games in 1928, aircraft from the *Langley* struck Pearl Harbor in a surprise attack. More stunning was the 1929 war game in which the *Saratoga* split from the rest of her battle fleet, swung around the Galapagos Islands, and surprised and the defenders of the Panama Canal as its aircraft "destroyed" the canal at daybreak.[124] *Saratoga* would, with some irony, execute a similar surprise attack against Pearl Harbor during war games in 1938. Doctrine, as such, was still unrefined as the capabilities of the carriers were explored.

The American commitment to naval aviation, by now understood to mean carrier aviation, remained strong throughout the 1930s. In 1930, with the United States already in the Great Depression, the Navy was authorized to lay down the hull of a "pure" carrier, the USS *Ranger*.[125] The *Ranger* was commissioned in 1934. In 1933 two carriers, the USS *Yorktown* and *Enterprise* were ordered; *Yorktown* was commissioned in 1937, *Enterprise* in 1938. The USS *Wasp* was ordered in 1935; the *Wasp* was commissioned in 1940.[126] The acquisition of these aircraft carriers represented an enormous investment for the nation and the Navy.

It must be remembered that aircraft carriers are useless without trained crews and accompanying aircraft. Thus the Navy simultaneously developed a series of aircraft designed for carrier operations. Perhaps the best remembered American carrier aircraft of World War II was the Douglas SBD Dauntless dive-bomber. During the May 7, 1942, Battle of the Coral Sea this aircraft was used to sink the Japanese carrier *Shoho*. At Midway on June 4, 1942, the carriers *Akagi*, *Kaga*, and *Soryu* were sunk by the crews using the Douglas Dauntless, with the *Hiryu* being seriously damaged.[127] These victories changed the balance of power in the Pacific. Entering the war in December 1941, how did the US Navy manage to have such a fine aircraft, with trained crews and pilots, in place by these battles? The Douglas Dauntless was conceived in 1938, building on lessons learned with earlier designs, like the Douglas TBD Devestator torpedo-bomber.[128] In fact, the American aeronautical industry in general was learning a great deal about the requirements of naval aircraft with the development of scout-bombers, torpedo-bombers, and dive-bombers ordered by the Navy during the 1920s and 1930s. The US Navy's development of attack aircraft reflects the doctrinal concept the Navy's leadership envisioned for aircraft carriers, not accident. Importantly, the carriers were by doctrine organized into "Battle Force, U.S. Fleet" and *not* into the "Scouting Force, U.S. Fleet."[129] The carriers were clearly seen as major surface combatants, not scouting vessels.

The mistaken evaluation of the US Navy on the eve of World War II is not unique and continues in professional literature and the popular press. The editor-in-chief of *U.S. News & World Report*, Mortimer B. Zuckerman, recently claimed that the interwar US Army persisted in the "silly strategy" of saving the horse cavalry long after tanks, machine guns, and barbed wire had rendered such cavalry useless.[130] Why did the Army's leadership insist on keeping the horse cavalry? Zuckerman states it was because "planners could not overcome the vested interests and pride of various arms of the military and their political sponsors." In fact, the interwar US Army was keenly interested in mechanized warfare, and struggled through the 1930s to fund experiments with mechanized forces. Experimentation, along with an observation of doctrinal development abroad, gave birth to early American mechanized doctrine. As the war in Europe began in 1939, the 1st and 13th Cavalry was already fully mechanized and had been combined into the technically advanced 7th Cavalry Brigade.[131] Through war games with such units, modern mechanized doctrine was established by the US Army before the Second World War began; the Army was simply waiting for permission to purchase the tanks and trucks required to fill mechanized divisions. Of course, no drawing board doctrine completely survives first contact with the enemy on the battlefield. Adjustments and refinements to American mechanized doctrine would continue through the war (and indeed, continues today).

## DECLINING FORCE STRUCTURES

As military organizations have become more dependent upon high technology equipment we can identify a trend toward smaller, though increasingly potent, force structures.[132] Although military use of new technologies is most visual in sophisticated weapons systems, important uses that effect military preparedness can be found in areas as far apart as payroll management to battle staff training.[133] In naval force structuring this translates to smaller fleets utilizing vessels that individually have impressive firepower. Indeed, the combined effect of these well armed vessels makes modern squadrons of ships more powerful than a fleet was a generation ago. This process has been underway for some time. In his work *Mass Armed Forces in Decline*, Manigant explains that numbers are increasingly less relevant than quality of equipment.[134] This concept is hardly new in warfare: small European expeditions colonized much of the known world through a military system of advanced weaponry and organization.[135] Through this military system British arms conquered and subjugated large regions like the Indian Subcontinent. Better organized societies, such as the Zulu people in Southeastern Africa, more effectively defended themselves against would-be colonizers; but in the end these societies also could not withstand the advanced weaponry of Western military units. As would be expected, the historic examples of superior arms defeating great numbers are numerous. The American Army is able to defeat native American Indian societies in the nineteenth century and halt the advance of numerically superior Chinese forces during the Korean War. Reverse examples, such as the Ethiopian success against better equipped Italian colonial forces on the eve of World War II, are rare. Allowing for such rare exceptions, we see that until taken to an extreme the superior size of a poorly equipped military organization can be effectively trumped by a numerically inferior opponent with advanced weaponry.[136] One effect of this development has been the increasing difficulty of measuring military capabilities among different nations. Just as the two million soldier strong Chinese People's Liberation Army is not widely considered to be the world's most capable army, so too will we reach the day when a measurement of gross naval tonnage no longer designates the world's most capable navy. When counting apples and apples—or something at least qualitatively approaching apples and apples—strength of numbers is still very important.[137] Comparisons of gross naval tonnage remain interesting and will no doubt continue to be evaluated some time to come. However, the impression given from comparisons of gross tonnage is increasingly irrelevant. Overall gross tonnage is still routinely used as shorthand to count the size/strength/capabilities of a fleet; for individual vessels it is said to imply the level of punishment that a vessel is capable of accepting before being rendered "combat ineffective." Increasingly though, such information is misleading if not coupled with information on ever changing fleet capabilities. Nations must strive not merely to keep adequate numbers (or tonnage) of warships afloat—the quality of the vessels afloat has become more important than numbers.

It is not just principal weapons platforms (whether they be ships, aircraft, or tanks) that are shrinking in number in modern force structures. The concentration on purely military specialties[138] within national armed forces is shrinking dramatically. This trend is most evident in the world's navies and air forces, but is also seen in armies. Janowitz points out that purely military occupational specialties in the US Army during the American Civil War stood at 93.2 percent—in the post-Korean War American Army they had fallen to 28.8 percent.[139] Such percentages of purely military specialties are even lower in the more technological services of the Navy and Air Force.

## THE RISKS OF COMPLACENCY

Victory is always preferable to defeat; and still, even success brings its own problems. Recent American success in the Cold War illustrates this point quite well. With the collapse of the Soviet Union a great victory was won by the West. However, amid this Cold War victory, the United States ironically lost something of value; something that the nation desperately seeks. As an adversary the Soviet Union forced America to excel—for half a century the United States focused its national energies to meet the Soviet challenge. Who would bury whom? The United States was obligated to define an ambitious international agenda, and was then forced to act upon that agenda. Would America have landed a man on the moon if the Soviet's had not been so adept in their role of antagonist and competitor? Maybe. But without a doubt the Soviets certainly pushed America into fits of greatness. Whether the Soviet threat was ever real, or merely imagined, is largely irrelevant now. The reaction to the threat became the reality.[140] With the challenge of communism the bipolarism of the Cold War became comfortable, or at least very familiar, to Americans; we knew our competition, and we were mostly confident that we could prevail. With the Cold War over the United States should attempt to reevaluate its international friends and adversaries with an eye to potential future competitors. As much as anything else, the US must fight the urge to become complacent after this significant success. Complacency for just a few years may cause irreparable damage to our national security as a nation may fall "generations" behind in technological development.[141] Sadly, such complacency is commonplace in history.[142]

In *Affording Defense* Gansler points out numerous problems with US weapons acquisition regimes that one would think only exist in an inept or complacent bureaucracy. Perhaps B. H. Liddell Hart's warning, mentioned in the introduction, about past success promoting complacency is already taking place in America. Of course, Hart is not alone in his concern. C. P. Snow considers the problems of a nation becoming trapped in a comfortable pattern; solutions to past problems (for example, American solutions to Cold War problems) are no longer relevant to emerging problems. Snow states

> More often than I like, I am saddened by a historical myth. Whether the myth is good history or not, doesn't matter; it is pressing enough for me. I can't help thinking of the Venetian Republic in their last half-century. Like us, they had once been fabulously lucky. They had become rich, as we did, by accident. They had acquired immense political skill, just as we have. A good many of them were tough-minded, realistic, patriotic men. They knew, just as clearly as we know, that the current of history had begun to flow against them. Many of them gave their minds to working out ways to keep going. It would have meant breaking the pattern into which they had crystallised. They were fond of the pattern, just as we are fond of ours. They never found the will to break it.[143]

The leaders of the Venetian Republic could not affect a new policy direction in time to save their republic. If successful nations do in fact risk becoming complacent, can they be overtaken by a hungry nation?

Issues of complacency become relevant to this study if dissatisfied nations seeking to upset the status quo are able to utilize technology to overcome their adversary. Lacking the conventional power to gain a favorable outcome, hungry nations will naturally seek unconventional alternatives; such unconventional alternatives may include "high tech" solutions to old power problems. This leads us to the question: Must transitions in relative technological expertise be accidental, or might they be driven? Lost in our general appreciation of scientific genius throughout history has been a recognition of the gifted scientist's ability to vary his investigative focus. Bronowski makes the point that scientific discovery can be directed:

> True, science is full of useful inventions. And its theories have often been made by men whose imagination was directed by the uses to which their age looked. Newton turned naturally to astronomy because

> it was the subject of his day, and it was so because finding one's way at
> sea had long been a practical preoccupation of the society into which
> he was born.[144]

This implies that societies can fruitfully direct their best minds to work in
specific areas of interest. Aron's observation (mentioned at the beginning
of this chapter), concerning a nation's ability to channel its available resources into military potential, is consistent with this line of thought. The
Allies relative success in this endeavor during World War II is an excellent
illustration of the point. In his classic *The Two Cultures and A Second
Look*, Snow describes the manner in which "a great many scientists had to
learn, for the good Johnsonian reason that sharpens one's wits, something
about productive industry"[145] during the Second World War. This precedent is important: given proper incentive, scientists and engineers can
successfully tailor their discoveries to assist a national war effort. Later
Snow claims that tradition and technical background appear to count for
very little in the harnessing of science into useful technology.[146] The lesson to be observed from this is that it is not terribly difficult for major nations to learn to become very good with technology. A people that desires
innovation in areas suited to an application of maritime power may
achieve a great deal of success. The claim that it is impossible, or at best
highly unlikely, for second-tier nations to uncover a scientific principle
that is difficult to comprehend will not dissuade them from making the attempt. It has long been noted that scientists as a group possess the characteristic of not believing that something is impossible until it has been
proven impossible.[147] Prodding, even controlling, technological innovation is much talked about in the sciences. For example, literature discussing technological research in medical sciences is full of examples of
technological advances being actively guided.[148] If innovation in medical
research can be managed, why not innovations in weapons research?

Issues of complacency are examined in society under the guise of
numerous terms. Popular today is the concept of "competitiveness"—or
more precisely, the concept of a growing lack of national competitiveness in the sciences and engineering. The number of scientists and technicians that a state produces has been directly linked to that state's
economic performance. Less industrially developed nations cannot afford to spend significant amounts of money on either scientific research
or technological development; they simply do not have the available capital. The significance of the non-industrialized world's research and development investment problem is dramatically shown when it is pointed

out that the developed world averages 2,875 scientists and engineers per million people, while less developed nations average only 121.[149] Thus, true technological competition exists only among the major industrially developed nations.[150] Consider American competition with other industrially-advanced nations like Japan: Americans are greatly concerned that their per capita number of scientists and engineers is low compared to their main economic competitors. The American versus Japanese problem is insignificant when compared to that of the Third World versus First World research and development obstacle. But will nations move to take military advantage of technologies that present themselves? Clearly some feel the answer is yes:

> Today, modest navies' admirals do not rely so much on Western experience as they used to. Usually younger and somewhat less "hidebound" than their Western counterparts, they are ready to take chances in order to step up their capabilities. In this regard, only those Western shipyards that will offer exotic but promising designs will be likely to beat their competitors. . . . Until recently, navies worthy of the name only numbered six or seven, of which only one or two were unchallenged at one time or another. Shipyards happily built whatever admirals requested without asking questions and all over the world, the "Admirals Union" ("the most powerful of all, except that of women's"—Winston Churchill) took great care not to introduce changes that would have disturbed the agreed balance of sea powers. . . . With such a potential backdrop for the future, the above factors combine to set up a "Revolution at Sea", a situation in which any contender feels free to put forward even the wildest concept.[151]

Rasler and Thompson note the returns on a given scientific of technological innovation diminish over time. Thus scientific and technological leads are by their very nature transitory. Unfortunately, nations currently enjoying a lead in technological prowess are apt to become complacent. This is perfectly understandable, since at their peak , these nations have little in the way of effective competition. When competition does reemerge, and it will, the response to the new challenge is apt to be both slow and clumsy. Institutional rigidities (formed during the period of dominance) emerge as an independent factor, and act as an additional brake on the pursuit of and effective policy for responding to the changing environment.[152] Rasler and Thompson conclude that their findings suggest a solid link between technological innovation, national power, and shifting international pecking orders.

International power rankings among the world's great powers are relatively stable. Occasionally through a burst of innovation, assuming the prerequisite supporting national potential, a nation catapults into a position of global dominance.[153] One area that can assist nations is developing a spirit receptive to new innovations is by altering the state's bureaucracies into organizations receptive of such developments. The successful use of technological innovation implies bureaucratic re-organization and administrative innovation. Nations address this issue differently due to their political culture and past success.[154] Large, complex organizations are required to create effective sea power—civil or naval. As Cohen suggests while considering air power in the Gulf War "The successes of the air campaign in the gulf rested almost as much on organizational innovations as on technology. To speak of a revolution in warfare as a purely technological affair is to miss half the significance of the war."[155] Much the same is true for the success of sea power. The British development of the HMS *Dreadnought* is an example of the British commitment, expressed in the organization of the naval bureaucracy, to the furtherance of sea power and maritime superiority. The development of the *Dreadnought* made obsolete not just foreign navies, but the British navy as well.[156] Rosen uses the British experience with the development of the tank in World War I and radar on the eve of World War II as other examples of successful bureaucratic outlook and organization.[157] Rosen suggests that the same organizational openness assisted the US Navy in developing doctrine for carrier operations and the US Marine Corps in developing doctrine for amphibious landings.

Military bureaucracy is not merely about procurement. Procurement is of itself a serious issue—what sort of bureaucracy is required to bring this off? The bureaucracy issue merges with the technological argument when it moves into restructuring and manufacturing.

## DRAWING BOARD TO FIELD

Gray tells us that states that are broadly technologically comparable will be able to register a military advantage in this area or that, but that technological superiority in a single (or even a superiority in several) weapons is not enough to forge victory.[158] The implication is that a collection of other military factors, such as an effective national strategy and well developed personnel training levels, are more important than the weapons systems used to fulfil said strategy or training. As a rule Gray makes an excellent point, but does this point not depend on the nature of the "one or even several weapons" which he envisions? More important yet is the use to which a new technology is put. Japan began the Pacific War with the use of advanced, low running torpedo technology at Pearl Harbor. Torpedo dive-bombings, thought impractical by the Americans in Pearl Harbor's shallow waters, brought the Japanese an important initial victory over the US Pacific Fleet. This advantage was relatively short-lived for numerous reasons, not the least of which being that a surprise use of a new technology, much like any other surprise, often only works once. Still, while it did not win the war for the Japanese, this new technology did provide the margin for an important early victory.[159] It is true that the Americans were vastly superior to the Japanese in industrial production capabilities during World War II, and still, the United States was not so far ahead technologically. In fact, the Japanese began the Pacific War with the most technologically advanced fighter in the Pacific Theater, and in the closing period of the war developed jet aircraft.[160] The substantial technological differential that separated the Japanese and the Americans was the development of atomic weapons. In fairness to Gray's generalization, he is not really speaking narrowly of technology, but also more broadly of industrial capabilities that put the given technologies to work. Even given this point, Gray is asserting that within the multitude of factors that influence victory or defeat in combat, technologically advanced weaponry counts for relatively little.

By definition, "technologically comparable states" that are roughly equal in technological and industrial capabilities do not have significant technological advantage over one another. But this simply raises the question of at what point such nations cease being comparable? Today, the United States and Japan are roughly comparable states in their degree of technological advancement and industrial capabilities. Consider two scenarios dealing with technological advances: If America were to develop (perhaps accidentally) a revolutionary breakthrough in artificial computer intelligence, would the two nations still be considered roughly equal technologically? This new American technology, once fielded, would make every computer-driven US weapon system, and US civilian and military industry generally, superior to anything the Japanese possessed. That superiority could well represent the margin of victory during war (or profit margins during peace). The real questions become: How long could the United States keep the new technology secret? And, How long would the process take from the drawing board to the fielding of the new technology in a weapons system? In this scenario the American response to the potential of the new artificial computer intelligence technology would be decisive. Even with otherwise industrially similar states, one or several technological advances could make a significant difference.

In a second scenario, both America and Japan develop the same artificial computer intelligence technology at the same time in a joint research endeavor. As with the first scenario, it is the response to the technological breakthrough that remains decisive. Would the American or the Japanese military leadership be the first to deploy weapons systems with this advancement? Based upon the decisions of industry leaders, would American or Japanese industry be the first to benefit from this innovation? Gray's observation that individual technological innovations among compatible nations has not yet proven decisive in combat is misleading for future strategists. It is true that battle's sometimes turn on strange and unforeseen twists of fate; however, many battle results are the predictable result of a better equipped, better trained, better led force defeating a weaker opponent.

It is said that in warfare everything is simple, but, that in warfare even the simplest things are difficult. It is a simple thing to desire equipping one's military force with weapons that are effective in combat. Today more than ever, this simple desire is a difficult task to fulfill. Thus nations that seek to compete at the highest international political and military levels must now seek expertise in all technological areas. Admiral F. N. Gromov, Commander of the Russian Navy, tells us that

> The development of modern navies is unthinkable without the application of the latest technology in shipbuilding, the creation of shipboard power and radio-electronic systems, infomatics, and also missile-artillery and mine-torpedo armaments. All of these are equally important for the Russian Navy, but among all of the promising technologies, the incorporation of newest achievements in the areas of microelectronics and computer equipment continues and will continue to have the most radical consequences in military affairs.[161]

Technological expertise must be broad and ever up-to-date.

The United States has made good use of its technological and industrial advantages for many decades. In *Affording Defense* Gansler points out that there are "two distinct categories" of military technological advances. The first category contains those advances that fit within the paradigm of the "military-industrial complex."[162] The second category of technological advancement is created by military R&D and is, according to Gansler, the more significant of the two categories. The second category involves "non-traditional" innovations that are brought about by a totally new type of weapon or weapon system. As a condition of being nontraditional, the new weapon breaks down some part of the traditional construct of the military-industrial complex paradigm. Gansler goes on to show why "a dialectic conflict" is created by this second category of technological innovations since both sides of the military-industrial complex resist the second category.[163] For example, the US Air Force is said to have institutional motives for resisting pilotless aircraft (like cruise missiles or reconnaissance drones) which serve to make pilots obsolete—thus the Air Force is said to resist developments in those areas.[164] Industry may also resist those developments in favor of more expensive manned aircraft. This dynamic is why we most often find technological advances that are merely improvements on existing systems, rather than bold new systems.

Part of the resistance to truly revolutionary technological advance is institutional rather than systemic; this is particularly true in successful (and complacent?) nations like the United States. If success tends to breed (or even to accommodate) some sort of complacency it is also likely that nations that have not enjoyed recent military success may be more open to nontraditional uses of technology. Consider even the limited example of the US Navy and "smart bombs" during the Gulf War. The US Navy came to resent the positive public attention given to US Air Force use of smart bombs. Before the Gulf War the Navy leadership maintained that smart bombs were a cost prohibitive strike option—Navy doctrine held that it was more cost effective to use multiple conventional bombs on a target. This doctrine was not well considered; multiple sorties creates a strain on naval service and support, on the crews flying the missions, and risks both crew and aircraft numerous times over the same target. The Air Force concept held that smart bombs, though expensive, were much cheaper than airplanes and their crews. Further, the Air Force wanted to know in time sensitive operations that there was a high probability that the target would be destroyed during the first attack. This Navy doctrinal failure during the war (albeit mostly a public relations failure since American armed forces had incredible success in the Gulf) has led the Navy to quickly rethink its armament composition.[165] Imagine the rethinking that would be going on within the US Navy if that institution had suffered worse than a public relations loss? After its Gulf War experience, is the leadership of the Iraqi Air Force likely more concerned with the traditional role of fighter pilots, or with victory over its potential adversaries through any effective weapon system? Iraq may be more willing then successful coalition nations to make revolutionary decisions regarding weapon development. Such a commitment to alternative weapons can not erase the deficiencies of the Iraqi industrial base, but does suggest that Iraq may through sacrifice achieve more of its military potential. Aron warns, "In wartime the degree of mobilization is chiefly a function of administrative capacity, but also, of the people's acceptance of sacrifice. . . . Lastly, belligerents wage war with actually mobilized, not potential forces."[166] Aron boldly asserts that organization (or "administrative capacity") is the key to realized ("mobilized") power. Aron assumes that in this regard national bureaucracies can be altered, particularly with the people's acceptance of sacrifice, in a manner that better facilitates the acquisition of military power. This explains the ability of an impoverished nation, like North Korea, to field an impressive military machine despite apparent national handicaps.

Satisfied nations may have difficulty understanding the drive of nations committed to reversing their fortunes. For institutional and bureaucratic reasons the United States may not be able to take full advantage of new ideas in design and procurement—other nations may not be so bureaucratically burdened. Gansler suggests that 'off-the-shelf' technology may provide an important technology source for those willing to escape the traditional weapon procurement system.

> And if proven, off-the-shelf commercial components were to be used, the DoD could acquire its electronic systems from 2 to 5 times more rapidly. Since most of today's weapon systems have between one-third and one-half of their cost devoted to electronics (and this ratio is growing), a shift to commercial components would make a dramatic difference in cost, quality, and schedule.[167]

Historically military research and development led to civilian applications. Pressing the aviation envelope for new fighter aircraft would give industry insight into better design options for passenger aircraft. Now, civilian research is beginning to generate military applications. What nation will be best at converting civilian technology to military use? Certainly not the United States. Most other industrialized nations have some sort of government agency (often civilian run) that attempts to create a synergy between civilian and military industrial research and development.[168] Gansler is not arguing for an American version of Japan's Ministry of International Trade and Industry (MITI), but he does see a need for some significant improvement in the American approach. For a number of historic reasons, the United States, ever opposed to such "industrial strategies," resists such government-private sector arrangements. To remain competitive in the emerging technological era, the DoD bureaucracy must change.

## RICH AND POOR NATIONS

Nations that industrialized early (symbolized by Britain, Germany, and the United States) have consistently maintained their relative technological lead over industrially developing latecomers. A hierarchy of economically successful states has been firmly established by industrialization—few states have made significant advancement toward the top of the hierarchy after beginning near the bottom. Notable exceptions to this rule are Japan, Taiwan, and South Korea. For the vast majority of economically unsuccessful states, their relative poverty appears to be permanent. Due to the geographic locations of these groups, the global economic division is commonly referred to as the North-South gap. Some states defy an easy placement into either the developed or non-developed categories. Nation-states like Russia, India, and China could conceivably be placed into an economically less developed category when they are compared with advanced states like Germany and Japan. Nonetheless, these states have overall economies and technological prowess this is light-years ahead of non-developed economic basket cases. Also, by comparison to many non-developed states, these states have relatively stable political institutions.[169]

People in developed states enjoy an average annual income of roughly $11,000—people in underdeveloped states average a dismal $190 annually. Citizens from industrialized nations like the United States can expect to live for about 76 years. Citizens from poorly industrialized nations can assume that they will live for just 52 on average.[170] One implication of the international economic system is that citizens of the non-developed states feel no compulsion to support the status quo. Indeed, they feel quite oppressed by the current political and economic world arrangement.

## SECOND TIER VS. FIRST TIER—INSTABILITY OF STATE POWER RANKINGS

In *Theory of International Politics* Waltz claims that nations "are not placed in the top rank because they excel in one way or another. Their rank depends on how they score on *all* of the following items: size of population and territory, resource endowment, economic capability, military strength, political stability and competence" (italics in original).[171] All industrially developed nations are not equally equipped; within this group there is an ever increasing rate of technological innovation may soon allow a "second-tier" maritime power to pass over a naval power that had been "first-tier" only months (or less) before. What sort of innovations are we talking about? Advances in propulsion, computer processing speed, artificial intelligence, communications, and new energy sources appear to offer nations vastly improved operational capabilities while simultaneously costing less in the form of production expenses. If weapon developmental costs can be kept in check through a shrewd (or even fortuitous) calculation of which technologies to emphasize, technologically competent nations may be able to seriously challenge first tier powers. In the past, technological superiority has provided important advantages unit for unit, but has been less important than overall numbers, tactics, and general national economic productivity. Mankind has reached a point in scientific and technological advancement where this dynamic may be turned on its head.

Individual technological innovations have always received a great deal of attention in conflict studies—an example of this attention would be the extensive examinations of the role the submarine played during World War I and World War II. Many scholars looking toward future conflicts inform us that collectively "information warfare" will be the next great contest between competing military applications of technology.[172] Current technological and engineering feats are captivating and important to digest. Russian efforts at developing torpedoes capable of 50–60 knots today, and up to 100 knots in the near future will no doubt revolutionize naval tactics.[173] But rather than examining a specific technological innovation on the horizon (or even a narrow spectrum of such innovations under the heading of information warfare), I will examine the phenomenon of an increased cumulative rate of technological innovation and its effects on the character of maritime power. Technological innovation has played a significant role in maritime power from ancient times—the character of ancient naval battles was forever changed with the advent of the ram and the grappling hook. Just as the ram and grappling hook gave Athenian navies an advantage over their adversaries, so too did the CSS *Virginia*[174] threaten to make obsolete the Union fleets enforcing the blockade on the Southern states during the American Civil War.[175] With the CSS *Virginia*, the Confederate Navy had developed a revolutionary change in its capabilities; where such developments once occurred sporadically, today such changes may occur almost overnight.

New technology has important commercial applications as well as naval applications. The nineteenth century American clipper ships utilized a novel sailing-mast design, which allowed American commercial interests to effectively compete as international cargo carries. More recently ro/ro cargo ships (named for their "roll on, roll off" loading and unloading capabilities) have challenged the cost effectiveness of many otherwise serviceable cargo ships. Because these innovations were modest (if still important) they could be countered or copied quickly by adversaries and competitors. Modern innovations have the potential to be both more decisive and more difficult to replicate.[176] As a result, the relative distance between the effectiveness of the great maritime powers and lesser sea-going nations will likely increase to a wide chasm.[177] That today's great maritime powers (all successful industrially relative to lesser states) may expand their maritime power relative to lesser states is important, though perhaps not surprising. Second, and more interestingly, the difference between first-tier and second-tier maritime powers within the great maritime powers is tenuous at best. Speed of innovation will compress to years—and may eventually compress to months—the relative advantage that it used to take decades to build.[178]

It does not require a navy that is superior in capabilities to the enemy's navy in order to be decisive strategically. In *A Naval History of England: The Formative Centuries*, Marcus suggests that a "well-handled mosquito fleet" can be decisive politically against a nation with a superior fleet if the smaller navy is deployed in a manner to achieve political, rather than strictly military, effect.[179] To illustrate his point, Marcus examines the strategies of the young American fleet while in operations against the dominant British fleet during the American Revolutionary War. In addition to a general campaign of *guerre de course* across all oceans, the American fleet engaged in specific naval actions that were designed to be politically embarrassing to the British rather than be militarily significant. The premier example of such successful actions occurred on September 23, 1779, when John Paul Jones captured a superior British frigate, the HMS *Serapis*, off the coast of England. Importantly, this night action took place on a moonlit night in the view of English crowds gathered on the cliffs of Scarborough and Bridlington.

The Chinese PLAN (Peoples Liberation Army's Navy) exemplifies the modern version of this philosophy. China's fleet has been described as a "naval guerrilla" force that embraces unconventional forms of warfare.[180]

While it is currently unlikely that the PLAN could militarily defeat a naval power like the United States, it could nonetheless inflict battle damage that would be *politically* unacceptable. Missiles, torpedoes, and mines are the PLAN's weapons of choice. Chinese doctrine proscribes the use of these weapons in naval ambushes, and from vessels concealed behind reefs or disguised as fishing vessels.[181] Even the recent purchase of Kilo submarines from Russia serve this doctrine since the Kilo-class comes with an integral mine-laying capability. The leadership of the US Navy will truly be remiss if it forgets its organizations own history against superior powers.

New technologies have certainly changed the operating capabilities of both merchant and naval ships; but, though tactics have changed, has maritime strategy necessarily changed its imperatives in war or peace? This analysis will build upon the body of research that has examined the role of new technology in warfare. The path to economic instability, caused by technological advances among economic powers, may demonstrate the future of strategic instability. The Swiss were known for generations for producing fine watches. To many, it seemed that Swiss domination of the international watch market was a permanent aspect of international life. When digital technology was introduced to the watch industry, the Swiss were not interested. The Swiss were convinced that such inelegant, if terribly precise, watches could never become a substitute for the elegance of Swiss moving parts. The Japanese led the charge to produce the new type of inexpensive, and highly reliable, watches. Swiss market share plummeted and has never fully recovered. These paradigm shifts representing new ways to look at technology and an existing product are nothing new. The American lack of interest in producing the VCR is well known, as is the story of the German loss of their position in the camera industry.

## NATURAL RESOURCE AVAILABILITY AND THE ROLE OF SEA POWER

This paper has already discussed how technological innovation and the post-Cold War international system may impact the character of sea power. The third projected change to the character of maritime power centers on the newfound ability to mine natural resources at sea. At stake is the possible obsolescence of the ancient notion that naval warfare is waged only to influence political events on land. Fighting at sea to control the political and economic disposition of the oceans—as opposed to the historic understanding of fighting at sea to impact political decisions on land—may occur for the first time in history due to newfound capabilities in the harvesting of strategically important resources from the sea. As deposits of natural resources grow scarcer on land, the attractiveness of ocean deposits will increase.

Part of the answer to the question of why nations put to sea lies in the degree to which geography makes a given nation dependent upon sea lanes for trade and security. There exists a natural geographic divide between those nations that must cross the water to do things, and those for whom it is an option. Nations such as the United States or Japan must travel across an ocean if they wish to impact a significant world power center[182] either militarily or economically. Other nations, like Russia or India, can reach numerous world power centers by land. But political geography can be deceiving. Pressure to secure now available economic resources will drive all great powers to the oceans, lest they miss the last great opportunity to make sovereign claim to uninhabited "land." If the oceans are indeed being divided between those nations with the ability to exercise maritime power, then all great powers will feel the pressure to act before everything is laid claim to.

The growing strategic importance of oil and other limited resources may expand the goals and responsibilities of maritime power in the direction of securing and defending portions of the oceans as if they were land. Naval war may become an end in its own right in our lifetime. Technology now allows man to remain "permanently" at sea—for example in durable oil rigs. While extreme storms can destroy these manmade objects, they are almost as secure as some highly populated areas on land that experience mother nature's lethal wrath with regularity. This newfound ability to inhabit and mine the sea has already led states to move for international recognition of their "exclusive economic zones" in the oceans. The extent and size of these economic zones is unprecedented when compared to the historic example of limited "territorial waters." Such economic zones could be interpreted as a precursor to an outright claim of sovereignty.

After fishing, the most significant resource currently taken from the ocean is oil. Technological advances in the last decade have revolutionized the ocean oil drilling industry. New detection gear has been combined with new mining equipment in efforts to probe depths impractical just a few years ago. Consider the example of the Gulf of Mexico: Because oil deposits in shallow water and close to shore were almost gone, this large body of water deemed "tapped-out" of oil by the industry until new technologies enabled oil companies to detect oil deposits 4,000 feet below the ocean's surface.[183] Until this decade it was difficult to locate oil more than 1,000 feet below the surface. Oil platforms operating in 2,500 foot waters are now the standard. In July 1996 the Shell Oil Company was drilling with tension-leg platforms in 3,000 foot waters. Drilling now occurs ever farther from the coast, and at ever increasing depths. In 1998 the Shell Oil Company anticipates deploying a tension-leg oil-production platform in 4,000 foot waters. Chevron has countered Shell with the development of a floating oil-production platform, the Genesis Spar. The Genesis Spar is already operating in 2,600 foot waters, and, because it is not tied to the ocean floor, it appears to have the potential for much deeper waters. Indeed, a consortium of oil companies (Shell, Mobil, Texaco, and Amoco) has begun exploratory drilling 200 miles off the Texas coast in 7,625 foot water.[184]

Accepting that in theory, new finds at sea of important natural resources might cause nations to jockey for the right to control those resources is one thing. Anticipating that real world trouble-spots will surface is another matter. Most students of international relations are aware of Chinese efforts to gain influence in the South China Sea region. Further, most are aware of the tremendous wealth in natural resources widely thought to lie beneath the waves in the South China Sea—these resources are thought to be every bit as important to the Chinese as any other strategic consideration. Fewer students of international relations have grasped the fact that the South China Sea region is not terrible unique in its projected wealth. The Gulf of Mexico, Gulf of Alaska, and the North Sea regions are all areas rich in petroleum reserves, and all are currently being tapped. From Galicia's Atlantic coast basin to the Pacific frontiers of Russia, oil and gas rich areas of the oceans are consistently being discovered.[185] It would seem that mankind is discovering enough reservoirs of important natural resources to cause many nations to make claims on the resources; however, nowhere near enough resources have been found to satisfy the needs of all nations.

Thus far in naval warfare it has been at best impractical, but more likely impossible, to exercise control over vast areas of the oceans. Commenting on the problems inherent in exercising such control, Gretton concludes the following: "So I would venture to suggest that while the establishment of fixed Maritime zones of control is welcome and desirable, it may not be practicable. But all is not lost. For the purpose of sailing ships or convoys, the essential need is to maintain temporary control in the vicinity of the ships which it is desired to move—a much easier task."[186] Gretton's comment speaks to a historic truth; technological advances and international accords are both working to change this.

## THE STRATEGIC IMPORTANCE OF NATURAL RESOURCES

"Often special metals or raw materials are needed for the production of war materials which cannot be obtained from the natural resources of the country. . . ."[187] This passage, written in 1920 as an explanation of why some nations feel compelled to develop sea power, remains valid today. The pursuit of secure sources of vital natural resources led Japan to covet Manchuria and the East Indies in the early twentieth century. The Japanese desire to control these areas led directly to Japanese involvement in World War II. From 1899–1902 Britain was willing to wage war to secure gold in South Africa (the Boer War). Whether we investigate the Spanish invasion of South and Central America centuries ago, or recent American military efforts in the Persian Gulf, we find an easy to follow chain of states engaging in warfare to secure vital, or simply profitable, resources. What has changed from the time of these historic examples is the present is the potential to harvest natural resources from the depths of the oceans. Some of these ocean "depositories" could eventually become strategic assets.

## TECHNOLOGY LEADING EXPLORATION

The exploration of new natural resource locations has long been tied to the value of the resource being sought. A rough cost of resource exploration and exploitation was weighed against the expected market value of the resource. This "cost versus benefit" approach to harvesting natural resources was economically appropriate in an era where exploration was highly expensive and imprecise. Petroleum exploration at sea, for example, had been both expensive and imprecise until the 1990s saw the increased use of 3D seismic technology.[188] Consider that in 1989 only 5 percent of the oil wells drilled in the Gulf of Mexico were based on exploration surveys utilizing 3D technology. Reductions in cost, refinement in 3D seismic technology that makes use of vertical instead of horizontal cable in acquiring 3D seismic data, coupled with the accumulation and processing of data acquired throughout the Gulf of Mexico between 1990 and 1993, has transformed the situation. In 1996 nearly 80 percent of oil wells drilled in the Gulf of Mexico were based on 3D findings.[189] Indeed, such technological advances have completely reinvigorated interest in mining for oil and gas deposits in the Gulf of Mexico. Discoveries today are occurring in relatively small deposit fields, fields that were too subtle to be found until recent advances in seismic data capturing technology was implemented in prospecting.[190] The Gulf of Mexico has been systematically mined for oil and gas since the 1950s.

Large oil deposits in relatively shallow water are now tapped, and one would expect that mining productivity would begin dropping. To reverse this trend, either a new exploration concept must be used, or new exploration technology must be used. In this case, new technology to explore has been coupled with advances in the mining process itself.

According to Clarance P. Ccazalot Jr., the vice-president of Texaco Inc. and the president of Texaco Exploration & Production Inc., today the two most critical factors affecting future American petroleum exploration are technology and personnel trained to use that technology.[191] Oil companies are now joined in major international competition to keep their competitive edge. The potential for new technologies in exploration of oil and gas deposits is great, as is the potential for the new application of existing technologies. For example, the use of radar in oil and gas exploration is receiving considerable attention in that industry.[192] Applying an existing technology to a new problem can be a difficult, but highly rewarding endeavor.

Curiously, one might think that the use of important new technologies would be dominated by major oil companies at the expense of smaller independents. In fact, since new technology is readily available to the independents, major producers have seen their relative advantage disappearing.[193]

## TECHNOLOGY CHANGING THE NATURE OF MARITIME POWER

In considering the principal difference between land warfare and sea warfare Brodie observes the following: "In war at sea there are no 'fronts,' no lines which are held by one side and besieged or attached by the other. A large body of water cannot be occupied in the sense in which land areas are occupied."[194] As an historic proposition Brodie's observation is accurate; sea power has always been associated with mobility and power projection. But what if Brodie is no longer correct? The precedent of attempting fortifications at sea, sea forts, is long established. New technologies may make this sort of development more cost effective and practical. Mallory and Ottar describe in *The Architecture of War* the British use of sea forts as fortified sea positions in the Second World War. These manmade islands were used primarily to extend the range of anti-aircraft artillery defending the United Kingdom. According to Posford, sea forts had the following objectives:

> 1. to break up enemy aircraft formations approaching a target such as London or Liverpool from the sea; 2. to prevent the laying of mines by

enemy aircraft in the navigable channels serving the great ports; 3. to prevent enemy E-boats carrying out raids on shipping and coastal targets in the estuaries; 4. to obtain early warning of the approach of hostile air or sea forces by means of radio location and direct telephonic communications with the shore; and by fulfilling 1, 2, 3, 4, to release for other duties the 'flak' ships which had hitherto patrolled the estuaries, and to provide the missing links in the chain of land defenses on either side.[195]

British use of sea forts in World War II was a success. With new technology readily available, today it is possible to establish such forts in deeper waters; and equipped with improved radar, sonar, artillery and missiles. The practical effect of freeing up the maneuver fleet would still apply— much in the same way that fortifications on land free the movement of the maneuver army. On land or sea fortifications are always more useful when used in conjunction with a maneuver element (the hammer and the anvil analogy is apt). Japanese use of islands in their defensive perimeter during World War II can be understood as utilizing natural sea forts. However, the Japanese maneuver fleet was incapable of maintaining communications with these islands. Isolated from the fleet, these island forts were defeated piece-meal or even left to wither in irrelevance as the US Navy advanced in other regions. Recollection of the last years of the Pacific War, when the Japanese Navy had already been broken, should not be allowed to cloud the strategic and operational problems that these island forts caused the US Navy while the Japanese Navy remained a viable power.

Although maritime power will be largely the purview of wealthy nations, it may offer some strategic advantage to small powers. For example, a nation with a marginal nuclear capability could theoretically use a disguised merchant vessel as an inexpensive, and obviously far reaching, launching platform.[196] This would be a 'low tech' solution to the 'high tech' and expensive problems posed by reliable ICBM or aircraft platforms. Conceptional, the idea of launching missiles from vessels goes back at least as far as World War II—earlier if one counts thrown projectiles as "missiles." Disguising combatants as simple merchant vessels is also not with precedent.

## CONCLUSION

Technological innovation has played, and will continue to play, a key role in the application of sea power. The important lesson would seem to be: Organizational receptiveness to innovative technology matters; organizational receptiveness to innovative technology varies. The receptiveness of organizations to technological change stems from many factors. Past success with innovations can create a "corporate attitude" that embraces the new. Conversely, past battlefield success without significant innovation can create an organizational environment that is suspicious of change. For those nations willing to embrace new technologies, and having the industrial and scientific infrastructure to make good this desire, the future will be a fluid (and possibly volatile) arena. Those nations unable or unwilling to pursue military applications of new technology will fall to second tier status, at best. However, the significance f weapons technology, though important, should not be overstated. Courage, leadership, and national will remain important intangibles in the application of military power; such intangibles serve to keep the outcome of warfare unpredictable.

## NOTES

74. Assertion based on interviews with three faculty members at Harvey Mudd College, September 18, 1996.

75. We must not confuse "accumulated knowledge" with wisdom. The ability to split the atom is a remarkable step in human societal progress. Mankind's ability to wisely utilize this knowledge is something else.

76. When considering this issue I think back to the many times in history that mankind has become convinced that somehow contemporary society (and often by extension contemporary man) has become superior to his ancestors. Sir Norman Angell's *The Great Illusion* (G.P. Putnam Books) claimed in 1910 that a general war in Europe was unthinkable. Europeans were too sophisticated now for such things, their national economies were too interconnected to allow for a general war, and besides, modern technology ensured that a general war in Europe would be too devastating to be seriously considered. Many wanted to believe that Angell was correct; moreover, they attempted to "prove" he was correct by various methods of quantifying his observations. Numbers derived as economic indicators appeared provoking on paper, but ultimately proved fallacious. Mankind and society had really not changed as much as Angell believed. Angell was not alone in his logic: in "Military Might," *National Review*, June 30, 1997, p. 40, John Hillen reminds us of the tradition of such thought in history. Hillen notes that Paine, Montesquieu, and Kant all shared Angell's basic belief that increased international trade and the growth of republics would guarantee lasting peace. With such examples in mind, I recognize that the perspective of those con-

templating the rate of technological and scientific advances in the late twentieth century may be skewed. The rate of technological innovation in society is superficially quantifiable (and thus "provable") in much the same way that economic indicators are quantifiable. Even given this, I remain convinced that it is possible to have an accurate, if unprovable, self-image of one's own society. For example, no doubt those living during the Renaissance were convinced that they had reached the height of human achievement—and in the fine arts and philosophy, perhaps they had.

77. J. Bronowski, *Science and Human Values*, 1965 edition, p. 7.

78. In "Military Effectiveness," *International Security*, Spring 1995, Stephen Rosen challenges this conventional wisdom. He suggests that India was in many ways technologically superior to Europe. Rosen suggests that military organization, perhaps a reflection of society, accounted for the British victory.

79. In *Asia's Next Giant*, 1989, Alice Amsden provides an excellent analysis of the transition from the First Industrial Revolution (undergone by Britain toward the end of the eighteenth century) to the Second Industrial Revolution (exemplified by Germany and the United States toward the end of the nineteenth century). Whereas the First Industrial Revolution was based upon invention, Amsden claims the Second Industrial Revolution was predicated upon innovation. Today Amsden claims that industrialization now occurs on the basis of learning.

80. General Charles Krulak, "Facing Westward to the Future," *Naval Institute Proceedings*, March 1997, p. 12.

81. The Toffler's devote a chapter to "The Knowledge Warriors" who reside in places like Silicon Valley. Their thesis is that clusters of high technology industries create groups of engineers and technicians whose military value is considerable, perhaps even decisive. In "America's Information Edge," *Foreign Affairs*, March/April 1996, p. 20, Joseph Nye and William Owens suggest that "the one country that can best lead the information revolution will be more powerful than any other. For the foreseeable future, that country is the United States."

82. Alvin Toffler and Heidi Toffler, *War and Antiwar*, 1993, p. 149.

83. Joseph Nye and William Owens, "America's Information Edge," *Foreign Affairs*, p. 20, and Eliot Cohen, "The Mystique of U.S. Air Power," *Foreign Affairs*, p. 122, respectfully.

84. Bernard Brodie, *Sea Power in the Machine Age*, 1941, p. 4.

85. Definitions of "science" and "technology" are offered later in this paper. Must a definition of "technology" include the industrial and engineering complex which brings new technology to fruit? And if yes, then why not also include a discussion of geography, population, political situation, etc., which also impact victory or defeat?

86. Alfred R. Hall, *Ballistics in the Seventeenth Century*, Cambridge at the University Press, 1952, p. 5.

87. See Sir Norman Angell's *The Great Illusion: A Study of the Relation of Military Power in Nations to Their Economic and Social Advantage*, 1910, for a classic example of a mistaken prediction of future short wars.

88. See Eliot A. Cohen's "The Mystique of U.S. Air Power," *Foreign Affairs*, January/February 1994, p. 109. Of course, other names exist for this paradigm shift. For example, Alvin Toffler and Heidi Toffler refer to this shift as "the third wave" in both *The Third Wave*, 1980, and *War and Anti-War*, 1993 (both books with Little, Brown and Company).

89. Eliot A. Cohen, "The Mystique of U.S. Air Power," *Foreign Affairs*, January/February 1994, p. 109.

90 Colin Gray, *Weapons Don't Make War*, University Press of Kansas, 1993, p. 176.

91. Found in Bernard Brodie's *Sea Power in the Machine Age*, 1941, p. 3. Jomini's suggestion that "Methods change, but principles are unchanging" seems to downplay the importance of advances in weaponry.

92. Timothy Garden explores these issues in depth in *The Technology Trap: Science and the Military*, Brassey's Defense Publishers, 1989.

93. See Irving Holley's "Doctrine and Technology as Viewed by Some Seminal Theorists of the Art of Warfare from Clausewitz to the Mid-Twentieth Century," p. 23. Found in *Emerging Doctrines*, 1988, Robert Pfaltzgraff et al, editors. Holley's examples show that sometimes new technologies are applied appropriately in weapons the first time.

94. See Edward Rowny's "Strategic Offense-Defense Mixes: The Impact of Arms Control," p 63, found in *Emerging Doctrines*, 1988, Robert Pfaltzgraff et al, editors. Rowny suggests that the battlefield gridlock that characterized World War I was broken through applications of new technology. In *Winning the Next War*, Cornell University Press, 1991, pp. 127–28, Stephen Rosen shows that the idea for the tank was first raised in November 1914. In April 1915 funding was received to develop prototypes, with the basic design being resolved in late June 1915. The first order for tanks was made in February 1916; this order was only fifteen months after the first conception. Granted, a proper understanding of the full range of operational and tactical uses for the tank took the British Army considerably longer, some forty months. As Rosen suggests, this delay did not stem from an unwillingness to try new technologies, but from a slowness of organizational learning. Importantly, such organizational deficiencies can be improved upon. An organizational culture supportive of innovation placed the British military in an excellent position to exploit the technological advances available to them during the World War II era. Further, and most importantly, although tanks

were used initially in World War I with little imagination—they were primarily used as mobile pill-boxes—they nonetheless were decisive in breaking the trench warfare stalemate.

95. Stephen Rosen, "New Ways of War," *International Security*, Summer 1988, p. 134.

96. The damage from these raids was very modest compared to the damage that strategic bombing would cause in the Second World War. Still, it was enough to receive the attention of the British government.

97. Indeed, it was this conclusion that led the British military to embrace the offensive concept to strategic bombing as a decisive weapon of war.

98. Irving Holley points out in "Doctrine and Technology as Viewed by Some Seminal Theorists of the Art of Warfare from Clausewitz to the Mid-Twentieth Century," p. 23, found in *Emerging Doctrines*, 1988, Robert Pfaltzgraff et al, editors, that German development of radar more or less paralleled British developments. Holley suggests that the key difference in actual use of radar in combat stemmed from perceived doctrinal need, which encouraged the British to push further with basic research.

99. Stephen Rosen, "New Ways of War," *International Security*, Summer 1988, p. 150.

100. See Kathleen Williams' *Secret Weapon: U.S. High-Frequency Direction Finding in the Battle of the Atlantic*, Naval Institute Press, 1996.

101. Found in *Cruise Missiles: Technology, Strategy, Politics*, The Brookings Institution, 1981, p. 3, Richard K. Betts editor.

102. In addition to the V weapons, the Germans had success in the development of high technology weapons like the Messerschmitt Me.262 jet fighter. Again, the German investment in jet fighters produced an impressive weapon that could only be decisive if deployed in significant numbers before the war was lost. The *Luftwaffe* understood the new jets, and used them appropriately when they received them in line units—however, by this point in the war the Germans no longer could produce such weapons in great quantity. In *Strategy for Defeat: The Luftwaffe 1933–1945*, Air University Press, 1983, Williamson Murray explains the irony of attaining such weapons too late to fully utilize their value.

103. The "Trinity Test" near Alamogordo, New Mexico, occurred July 16, 1945. Hiroshima was bombed August 5, 1945 and Nagasaki was bombed August 9, 1945. Found in *Operation Crossroads: The Official Pictorial Record*, 1946, p. 7. Even considering the Manhattan Project's time frame as encompassing Einstein's letter to FDR where he first outlined a possible use of the atom in a weapon still demonstrates a remarkable feat.

104. Found in Lawrence Freedman's *War*, Oxford University Press, 1994, p. 121.

105. Found in Timothy Garden's *The Technology Trap: Science and the Military*, 1989, p. 7.

106. Appendix A provides a table of emerging technologies that the US National Research Council has deemed important to national security. The National Research Council, at the request of the US Army, created a committee on "Strategic Technologies for the Army of the Twenty—first Century" (STAR 21). The provided table highlights that committee's projections of technologies that may offer decisive advantage when deployed in weapons on the battlefield.

107. Bernard Brodie, *Sea Power in the Machine Age*, 1941, p. 10.

108. John Terrain, *The U-Boat Wars*, G. P. Putnam's Sons, 1989, p. 158.

109. Recall that the US Navy had begun equipping vessels with anti-aircraft batteries in World War I.

110. See Robert Stern's *The Lexington Class Carriers*, Naval Institute Press, 1993, p. 12.

111. *Jane's Fighting Ships*, 1919, pp. 123–128.

112. German Zeppelins engaged in bombing and observation missions from Paris to London. British large aircraft carriers attempted to close with Zeppelins seen moving over the Channel, but the Zeppelins, upon seeing the carriers, would flee before the carriers were within range to launch aircraft. In 1918 a small barge (called a lighter) was equipped with a flight deck and a single Sea Camel fighter. The barge was towed into the Channel by a destroyer. The speed of the destroyer, 30 knots, helped give the Sea Camel lift since its flight deck was only 30 feet long by 15 feet wide. A German Zeppelin investigating radio traffic in the Channel approached the barge not realizing its danger. The aircraft was successfully launched, and the British pilot managed to shoot down the Zeppelin. See Timothy Kutta's "Captain Charles R Samson would not give up on his idea to use a towed barge as an aircraft carrier," *Aviation History*, May 1997, pp. 10 and 62.

113. Indeed, the leadership of the US Navy would also have been familiar with developments regarding airplanes and land warfare. In the World War I order of battle, German armies and corps were each allotted one integral Flying Detachment (or *Flieger Abteilung*) or twelve airplanes. Allied formations operated with attached air squadrons. For more information, see Brigadier-General Sir James E. Edmonds' *Military Operations: France and Belgium, 1914*, MacMillam and Co. Ltd., 1933, pp. 485–498.

114. *Aviation in the United States Navy*, Naval History Division publication, U.S. Government Printing Office, 1965, p. 1.

115. *Aviation in the United States Navy*, Naval History Division publication, U.S. Government Printing Office, 1965, p. 5.

116. Recall that the U.S. Navy was deeply influenced by Mahan's writing. Through this conceptual construction, in World War I the clashing commercial

interests of Germany and Britain were viewed as a significant cause of the war. Britain, with the stronger navy, was able to protect its sea lines of communication; the Germans, with an inferior navy, became isolated and lost the war. Rising American global economic interests raised the possibility of conflict with both Japan *and* the United Kingdom. See Stern's *The Lexington Class Carriers*, 1993, p. 11, for a discussion of this concept.

117. The Washington Naval Conference, 1921–22, authorized the famous 5–5–3 battleship ratio for the United States, Britain, and Japan. Significantly, the naval establishment considered this treaty obligation to be based more on political posturing than military sense. For example, Rear Admiral Bradley A. Fiske poses the question "Will airplanes make the 5–5–3 battleship ratio worthless in a few years?" as the basis of his article "The Strongest Navy," *Current History*, July 1922, pp. 557–63. The fact that Navy personnel were skeptical of the merit of the Washington Conference is further evidenced later that year as William Howard Gardiner wrote "The Philippines and Sea Power," *North American* Review, August 1922, pp. 165–173, and Commander C. C. Gill wrote "The New Far East Doctrine," *Naval Institute Proceedings*, September 1922.

118. In March 1919 the US Navy conducted a series of tests where the battleship USS *Texas* conducted firing exercises with the aid a spotting aircraft. The results of this test convinced even the most stubborn American opponents of naval air warfare that naval aviation, and by extension the aircraft carrier, was the future of naval warfare. Past ideas to use sea-planes for aerial spotting would be unworkable since an enemy fleet equipped with lighter and more maneuverable wheeled aircraft would simply shoot down US sea-planes, and thus gain control of the sky. Control of the sky, if for no reason other than aerial spotting for the battleships, was understood to mean effective control of the battle. Robert Stern's *The Lexington Class Carriers*, 1993, p. 19.

119. The original name of the vessel was the USS *Jupiter*, laid down in 1912. Found in *Jane's Fighting Ships*, 1931, p. 468.

120. The US Navy was behind the Royal Navy in the development of large aircraft carriers primarily because early American efforts in naval aviation centered on sea planes rather than wheeled planes. Indeed, this was not a completely unreasonable direction to begin, though the advantages of carrier based aviation soon became apparent. Robert Stern's *The Lexington Class Carriers*, 1993, p. 15.

121. *Jane's Fighting Ships*, 1931, pp. 316 and 319.

122. *Jane's Fighting Ships*, 1931, p. 466. These two carriers were originally, in 1916, intended to be battle cruisers of 35,300 tons. Unable to secure funds for a "pure" carrier program, the Navy decided to alter these vessels. Each carrier, with aircraft, nonetheless represented a $45,000,000 investment. The conversion

of these vessels was not exceptional. The Japanese converted a 42,000 ton battle cruiser into a carrier—the *Akagi* was completed in 1925.

123. Izetta Robb's "Navy's First Ace," p. 82. Found in Van Wyen's *Naval Aviation in World War I*, 1969. Van Wyen is the Historian, Deputy Chief of Naval Operations (Air).

124. In a tactical first, *Saratoga's* aircraft were launched while it was still dark, in an effort to time their appearance over the Panama Canal with daybreak. Ernest McNeil Eller, *The Soviet Sea Challenge*, p. 37.

125. *Jane's Fighting Ships*, 1931, p. 467. The *Ranger* was intended to be completed in 1934, so the Navy did accept a lengthy building process in order to win congressional support for this vessel. Again, lessons learned in operations with older carriers (the *Lexington* and *Saratoga*) were incorporated into the new design. In *The Soviet Sea Challenge*, Cowles Book Company, p. 37, Ernest McNeill Eller points out that the Navy Department had requested funds to construct five carriers; however, Congress would only authorize the funding of a single carrier with construction costs spread over a few years.

126. James Fahey's *The Ship's and Aircraft of the United States Fleet*, seventh edition, Naval Institute Press, 1988, p. 9.

127. Enzo Angelucci and Paolo Matricardi, *Complete Book of World War II Combat Aircraft*, Military Press, 1988, p. 254.

128. The Douglas TBD Devastator was originally designed in 1934, going into fleet service in 1937. Though a sound design on paper (an all metal low wing monoplane with retractable landing gear), this aircraft was truly obsolete by the beginning of World War II. During the Battle of Midway fourteen of fifteen Devastators flying off the *USS Hornet* were easily shot down by the Japanese as they attempted to attack Japanese carriers. These early version aircraft were pressed into service due to insufficient numbers of modern aircraft. See Enzo Angelucci and Paolo Matricardi's *Complete Book of World War II Combat Aircraft*, 1988, p. 252.

129. James Fahey's *The Ships and Aircraft of the United States Fleet*, 1988, p. 27.

130. Mortimer B. Zuckerman, "Winning the future's wars," *U.S. News & World Report*, May 12, 1997, p. 83.

131. Shelby L. Stanton, *World War II Order of Battle*, Galagad Books, 1984, p. 21.

132. Indeed, even the popular press has noticed this trend. In "The high-tech cavalry" article of June 28, 1993, *U.S. News & World Report*, Auster notes that the Pentagon has been forced to depend on advanced technology to offset declining force structures as it contemplates fighting two major wars at roughly the same time.

133. The American military has found that computer simulators can be both realistic and an excellent means of stretching limited budgets (after a large initial investment). See "New Weapons of War," *U.S. News & World Report*, May 31, 1993, and Elroy Garcia's "Modern technology updates the spirit of the Louisiana Maneuvers," *Soldiers*, September 1993, for analysis of this trend. Indeed, Jacques J. Bally points out in "The Shape of Ships to Come II," *Armada International*, February/March 1996, that standard policy now dictates that prior to any procurement or change in tactics all services in the US Armed Forces must run a series of war games on computers to test expected gains. Nations with superior technology will enjoy superior weapons, superior simulators for their soldiers to train with, and may even enjoy a pay management system that allows soldiers to worry about the battle at hand instead of worrying about whether the pay check will arrive home in time for the family to buy groceries.

134. Found in Lawrence Freedman's *War*, 1994, p. 131. Philippe Manigant is not saying that numbers are not still important in a contest between like forces; he is simply stating that a significant qualitative equipment edge is today more decisive than significant weight of equipment or troop numbers.

135. Note that the advanced military organizations of the European powers would have been largely irrelevant, and perhaps even counterproductive, without the modern weapons that precipitated such organizational change. German advances in the creation and organization of military staffs may be beneficial to almost any military force. However, specific changes in the organization of the fighting element, say the infantry company, are predicated on the introduction of new weapons. Dividing infantry companies into platoons, platoons into squads, and squads into teams, only makes military sense if these elements have the capability to accomplish tasks independently. A six man infantry team has significant firepower with the advent of quick-firing, long-range rifles. An attempt to implement such an organization in a force that lacks such weapons would prove disastrous. It would be foolish for soldiers equipped only with sword and spear to attempt to form squads or teams. Thus, in many respects military organizations can modernize only as the tools available to the military force modernize.

136. Obviously the political will to do whatever is required to win can become decisive if the combatants are worlds apart in this important realm. American forces held a vast technological superiority over North Vietnamese forces (despite a serious effort on the part of the Chinese and Soviets to offset this technology imbalance) and nonetheless lost the Vietnam War. Simply put, the North Vietnamese people and political leadership were much more steadfast than their American counterparts.

137. I am not suggesting that any technological superiority translates to victory over a numerically superior enemy force. During the Cold War the United

States military deployed numerous weapons systems that were, one for one, superior to the weapons systems of their Soviet counterparts. This is not to suggest that the Soviet equipment was poor, when, in fact, it was often quite good. The result was that since the American qualitative edge in weaponry was modest, though present, the United States still had to remain concerned about the vast size of the Soviet armed forces. A single American tank might be reliably counted on to defeat a single Soviet tank in battle, but that same tank could not be counted upon to defeat four Soviet tanks.

138. By "purely military specialties" I refer to combat specialties as opposed to combat-support or combat-service-support specialties. Thus an infantryman or a field artilleryman engages in a purely military specialty. A military police officer engages in a combat-support role. An Army cook, while still a uniformed service member contributing to the war effort, operates in a combat-service-support specialty.

139. Janowitz, *The Military Professional*. Found in Lawrence Freedman's *War*, 1994, pp. 124–5.

140. In *After Bipolarity*, The University of Michigan Press, 1995, Fred Chernoff reminds us that according to realists like Wolfers (in *Discord and Collaboration*, 1962) and Walt (in *The Origins of Alliances*, 1987), the perception of a common threat will serve to promote cooperation among members of an alliance (3). Chernoff suggests that "The existence of a threat is not a necessary condition of alliance cooperation; nevertheless, threats help" (2). We can thus continence the argument that the Soviet threat not only galvanized a Western commitment to resist Soviet advances—especially advances in Europe—it further encouraged a sense of purpose in America.

141. Technological generations no longer take the equivalent of a human generation. Computer technology illustrates the speed with which new "generations" now come and go; the state-of-the-art "generation" may change more than once a year.

142. See Karen Rasler and William Thompson's "Technological Innovation," *The Journal of Conflict Resolution*, September 1991, for an analysis of this trend.

143. C. P. Snow, *The Two Cultures*, Cambridge University Press, 1987 edition, p. 40.

144. J. Bronowski, *Science and Human Values*, Harper and Row Publishers, 1965 edition, p. 7.

145. C. P. Snow, *The Two Cultures*, 1987 edition, p. 33.

146. C. P. Snow, *The Two Cultures*, 1987 edition, p. 45.

147. This argument is made by C. P. Snow in *The Two Cultures and A Second Look*, 1987 edition, p. 7. It is not enough for many, or even most of us, to

think something will not work. As long as some possess the will to try, these few just might find a way to may the implausible possible.

148. See Steven R. Eastaugh's "Financing the Correct Rate of Growth of Medical Technology," *Quarterly Review of Economics and Business*, pp. 54–60, Vol. 30, No. 4, Winter 1990. Also see Richard Southby and Warren Greenberg, editors, *Health Care Technology under Financial Constraints*, Battelle Press, 1987, found Eastaugh's article.

149. Found in Dennis Pirages' *Global Technopolitics: The International Politics of Technology and Resources*, Brooks/Cole Publishing Co., 1989, p. 144.

150. As has been discussed elsewhere in this paper, a requisite amount of industrialization is required of nations if they seek to compete with the technological innovations of nations utilizing well developed industrial bases. It is true that in non-developed nations brilliant individual scientists and technicians may make fascinating, and important, discoveries without the benefit of an industrial base from which to draw support. Nonetheless, a lack of industrial base will work to retard the ability of a nation to compete effectively in high technology innovations.

151. Jacques Bally's "The Shape of Ships to Come II," *Armada International*. February/March 1996, 1/1996/E, p. 7.

152. Karen Rasler and William Thompson, "Technological Innovation," *The Journal of Conflict Resolution*, September 1991, p. 420.

153. Karen Rasler and William Thompson, "Technological Innovation," *The Journal of Conflict Resolution*, September 1991, p. 424. Obviously there are other ways to be catapulted into a higher international ranking. Shrewd strategic insight, or gross strategic misconduct by opponents, can provide the margin for a transfer of relative position.

154. A rich literature regarding the significance of social and culture differences in strategic studies has been developing since the early 1980s. See Alastair Johnston's "Thinking about Strategic Culture," *International Security*, Spring 1995, Stephen Rosen's "Military Effectiveness: Why Society Matters," *International* Security, Spring 1995, Richard Pipes' "Why the Soviet Union Thinks It Could Fight and Win A Nuclear War," *Commentary*, July 1977, Colin Gray's "National Styles in Strategy," *International Security*, Fall 1981 and his *Nuclear Strategy and National Style*, Hamilton Press, 1986. I am indebted to Johnston, p. 32, for exposing me to the last three sources.

155. Eliot Cohen, "The Mystique of U.S. Air Power," *Foreign Affairs*, January/February 1994, p. 116.

156. This irony is well documented and much commented upon. I recommend Bernard Brodie in *A Layman's Guide to Naval Strategy*, 1942, p. 29, for a useful analysis of this issue.

157. Stephen Rosen, "New Ways of War," *International Security*, Summer 1988.

158. Colin Gray, *Weapons Don't Make War*, 1993, p. 109.

159. The early string of victories were crucial to the Japanese strategy of creating a large buffer zone in the Central and Western Pacific around which they would attempt to consolidate and fortify a defensive perimeter. A strategic defensive posture would be assumed for the remainder of the conflict. The Japanese assumption was that the United States would tire of a prolonged and costly Pacific campaign was not completely unfounded. By the time America was ready to invade the Japanese home islands, the US government was looking for almost any means to avoid the casualties that such an invasion would entail. The Soviet Union was offered much in Europe as an inducement to lend its manpower to the invasion (John Lewis Gaddis in *Strategies of Containment*, Oxford University Press, 1982, speaks of a figurative deal with "the devil," the Soviet Union). In the end the atomic bomb saved the United States from either a deal with the Soviets or terrific losses.

160. The Mitsubishi A6M, or Zero as it became better known, was the dominant fighter in the Pacific Theater at the beginning of World War II. The Battle of Midway broke the air superiority that this remarkable aircraft had helped Japan gain. The Nakajima Kikka jet bomber project was based upon the German Messerschmitt Me.262 project. The Japanese had also made an early attempt at a jet fighter loosely based upon the Messerschmitt Me.163 B program. Although neither of these jet aircraft seriously impacted the air war, they do demonstrate the level of technological expertise of Japanese aeronautical engineers. Source is the *Complete Book of World War II Combat Aircraft* by Enzo Angelucci and Paolo Matricardi, 1988, pp. 321 and 344.

161. Admiral F. N. Gromov, "The Russian Navy's Commander Responds," *Naval Institute Proceedings*, June 1996, p. 47.

162. Gansler's use of the phrase "military-industrial complex" is conventional. He assumes that the military authorities purchasing weapons and the industrial authorities building those weapons have come to develop a tacit understanding that neither side will "rock the boat." That is, neither the military nor industry authorities desire a real change in the status quo.

163. Jacques Gansler, *Affording Defense*, The MIT Press, 1991, pp. 215–218.

164. Air Force resistance to cruise missiles and pilotless drones is widely accepted in literature dealing with weapons acquisition. Although there is some truth to the suggestion that the Air Force is institutionally committed to retaining its pilots, it should not lightly be assumed that the Air Force is therefore against pilotless forms of aircraft. This issue is reminiscent of the US Navy before the

Japanese attack at Pearl Harbor. To this day pre-World War II Navy leaders are accused of neglecting the role of the aircraft carrier in favor of the familiar battleship. The historic evidence disputes this myth. The US Navy was immensely interested in the potential of aircraft carriers as early as the 1920s. In *The U-Boat Wars*, 1989, John Terraine shows that in 1910 the US Navy successfully launched an aircraft from a cruiser. In 1911 the Navy was successful at landing and taking off of the USS *Pennsylvania*. Naval war games in the Panama Canal region in 1928 demonstrated the offensive strike capability of aircraft carriers (and an evolved appreciation of operational art) when the USS *Langley* split away from the "attacking" naval task force and successfully approached the Isthmus of Panama undetected by the defending forces. The carrier launched a dawn attack on the Canal that was credited with "destroying" the objective. Low funding levels from a government locked in the Great Depression, not an unrealistic vision of the future of naval warfare, caused American naval forces to be initially unprepared for the Japanese threat.

165. See Thomas Parker's essay "The Navy Got It: Desert Storm's Wake-Up Call," *Naval Institute Proceedings*, September 1994, for analysis of this phenomena. Also see "Reaching Globally, Reaching Powerfully: The United States Air Force in the Gulf War," a Department of the Air Force publication (September 1991) that stresses the importance of smart bombs in the Gulf War, and further stresses that it was the US Air Force that fielded the vast majority of these munitions.

166. Raymond Aron, *Peace and War*, 1966, p. 63.

167. Jacques Gansler, *Affording Defense*, 1991, p. 232.

168. For an analysis of this, see Jacques Gansler, *Affording Defense*, 1991, p. 275.

169. The current political instability of Russia is accepted and is an exception.

170. Dennis Pirages, *Global Technopolitics*, 1989, pp. 145–6.

171. Kenneth Waltz, *Theory of International Politics*, 1979, p. 131.

172. George Kraus seems to capture the spirit of this argument with "Information Warfare in 2015," *Naval Institute Proceedings*, August 1995. Generally, information warfare has two aspects. First, it attempts to fight the fog of war by providing friendly forces with accurate and timely information regarding operational status. It is in this spirit that General Krulak, the Marine Corps Commandant, recently stated "the junior enlisted Marine is going to have access to, and the need to use, more information than a battalion commander might today." Quote found in F. G. Hoffman's "The U.S. Marine Corps in Review," *Naval Institute Proceedings*, May 1997, p. 91. Second, information warfare attempts to deny useful information to the enemy. For example, a computer virus might be

placed into the enemy's computer information net with the expectation of degrading the effective flow of information.

173. "Why Not 100 Knots." *Naval Institute Proceedings*, November 1996, p. 88.

174. The ship is also known by its prior Union name of *Merrimack*.

175. This appeared possible for a short time following the initial Confederate victory with the CSS *Virginia* over four wooden hulled Union warships. The US Navy of course countered the CSS *Virginia* with the USS *Monitor* in the indecisive battle at Hampton Roads on March 9, 1862. Though tactically a draw, the engagement at Hampton Roads was a strategic victory for the Union. Had the Union fleet been rendered obsolete, the Union blockade of the South would have been in jeopardy. Confederate naval forces were in no position to accept a draw that merely reinforced the status quo—the Confederate Navy needed a victory, and it was unable to win that victory at Hampton Roads.

176. Obviously, innovation alone is not enough. The proper and early application of new technologies, whatever their potential, is as important as the development of the technology in the first place.

177. In *The Two Cultures* C. P. Snow claims that the main issue of the scientific revolution was that "the people in the industrialized countries are getting richer, and those in non-industrialized countries are at best standing still: so that the gap between the industrialized countries and the rest is widening every day" (41). The concept of a profound global scientific and technological division is well established.

178. For example, while the British might have looked across the Channel and feared growing German naval power in the early twentieth century, an actual German maritime power transition would take decades to achieve. By the time World War I had begun, Germany had actually surpassed Britain in the strategically important area of steel production. The steel industry is relatively static when compared to a strategically important modern industry, like computer chip production. A revolution in computer chip design can take place in mere weeks or months, rather than at the comforting pace of decades.

179. G. J. Marcus, *A Naval History of England: The Formative Centuries*, Little, Brown and Company, 1961, pp. 417–421.

180. Barry Blechman and Robert Berman, *A Guide to Far Eastern Navies*, Naval Institute Press, 1978, p. 107.

181. John W. Lewis and Xue Litai, *China's Strategic Seapower*, Stanford University Press, 1994, p. 222.

182. Kennan argued that only five world military and economic power centers had the requisite human and industrial potential to mount the sort of amphibious endeavor that could threaten the security of the United States.

183. "Oil giants tap Gulf depths: New technology opens a field of their dreams," *Sacramento Bee*, Tuesday, April 30, 1996, p. C1 and Chris Kraul, "A Spar is Born: Advances Let Oil Firms Go Where No Drill Has Gone Before," *Los Angeles Times*, Monday, February 17, 1997, p. D1.

184. "Oil giants tap Gulf depths: New technology opens a field of their dreams," *Sacramento Bee*, Tuesday, April 30, 1996, p. C3.

185. For more information see "Galicia's Atlantic coast basin—A new oil province?" in the March 28, 1994 issue of *Oil & Gas Journal* and "Potential of Pacific frontiers of former Soviet oil, gas empire" in the April 25, 1994 issue of *Oil & Gas Journal*.

186. Peter Gretton, *Maritime Strategy*, 1965, p. 23.

187. Kennan argued that only five world military and economic power centers had the requisite human and industrial potential to mount the sort of amphibious endeavor that could threaten the security of the United States.

188. 3D visualization technology helps geoscientists analyze salt layers in the ocean floor. The salt's geometry and emplacement history can then be considered before mining locations are established. For a description of this technology, and others now improving the success rate of ocean mining, see John Miers' "Technology Gives Gulf Prospects World-Class Investment Appeal," *Oil & Gas Journal*, January 20, 1997, p. 54.

189. See "U.S. E&P surge hinges on technology, not oil price," *Oil & Gas Journal*, January 13, 1997, p. 42.

190. See John Miers' "Technology Gives Gulf Prospects World-Class Investment Appeal," *Oil & Gas Journal*, January 20, 1997, p. 50.

191. See "U.S. E&P surge hinges on technology, not oil price," *Oil & Gas Journal*, January 13, 1997, p. 42.

192. See Thomas Bailey's "Application of X-band Radar to Sense Hydrocarbon Seepage," *Oil & Gas Journal*, December 9, 1997, p. 72.

193. See "U.S. E&P surge hinges on technology, not oil price," *Oil & Gas Journal*, January 13, 1997, p. 42.

194. Bernard Brodie, *A Layman's Guide to Naval Strategy*, 1942, p. 84.

195. This quote was found in Keith Mallory and Arvid Ottar's *The Architecture of War*, Pantheon Books, 1973, p. 137. The authors credit Posford's *The Construction of Britain's Sea Forts, The Civil Engineer War*, Volume 3, p. 33, as their source.

196. "Sea delivery: a rogue state's third option," *Jane's Intelligence Review*, May 1996, Volume 8, Number 5, p. 236.

# CHAPTER 3

# National Merchant Marines and Economic Reliance on Sea Power

*If the chief purpose of a navy is control of sea-
borne transportation, the vehicles of such transportation must be considered not as incidental
to sea power but as an essential part of it. . . .
A locomotive without cars attached represents
power well enough, but power without func-
tional meaning. . . . for a hostile fleet may fre-
quently be evaded, but the consequences of a
shortage of shipping can not be evaded.*[197]
—BERNARD BRODIE, *A LAYMAN'S GUIDE
TO NAVAL STRATEGY*

## MARITIME POWER AND TRANSPORTATION

As stated in Chapter 1, the use of ships as platforms for fishing was likely
the initial reason that early man built his first vessels. While fishing remains an important economic activity, the transport of men and material
quickly surpassed fishing in economic, and especially military, importance. For centuries, then, sea power has been fundamentally the power
of transportation. This fundamental aspect of sea power has not changed,
though other aspects of sea power appear to be in the process of emerging. The traditional characteristic of sea power is being transformed
today as technological advances allow an unprecedented harvesting of
natural resources from the oceans (see Chapter 2 for a detailed discussion of this trend). The importance of the collection of natural resources,
still including fish, can only increase. Despite the suggested evolution in
the characteristic of maritime power, transportation remains the essential
characteristic.

Without effective transport capabilities sea power can, at best, act
only as a negative influence upon an opponent; that is, naval power can
only be used to deny ocean-borne transportation to the enemy. In some
scenarios even this negative influence upon the enemy could be strategi-

cally decisive if the enemy were disproportionately dependent upon sea transport. When considering classic confrontations between continental and maritime powers we find that the ability of the continental power to deny sea-borne transport of goods, equipment, and personnel to the maritime power strikes at the heart of the sea power. Thus, in both World Wars the continental Germans attempted to deny the maritime British freedom of action on the high seas—the German failure in this endeavor was a vital component of Germany's ultimate defeat in both conflicts. Similar examples, demonstrating successful or incomplete denial of sea passage, flow throughout recorded history. When continental Rome successfully disrupted maritime Carthage's freedom of action in the Mediterranean, Roman victory became a forgone conclusion in the Punic Wars. Importantly, it is not just continental nations that attempt to attack maritime nations at their center of power. In the Second World War the maritime United States confronted maritime Japan in a conflict waged across the vastness of the Pacific Ocean. From the beginning of the Pacific War the United States sought to destroy, interrupt, and otherwise defeat the Japanese merchant marine. The catastrophic Japanese merchant marine losses during that war were every bit as strategically important as Japanese losses of naval vessels. Perhaps it is institutional recollection of this fact that has led the modern US Navy into a reconsideration of its current sealift doctrine and capabilities. Consider the following statements on sealift made in a recent US Navy and Marine Corps White Paper:

> Beyond the shift in emphasis of the Naval Forces, there are some traditional naval missions for which we must redouble our efforts to improve our capability. Of particular importance, sealift is an enduring mission for the Navy. Our nation must remain capable of delivering heavy equipment and resupplying major ground and air combat power in forward crisis. Sealift is the key to force sustainment for joint operations, and we are committed to a strong national sealift capability.[198]

It was beyond the scope of "... From the Sea" to recommend specific force structures to fulfill this "enduring mission for the Navy." We are therefor left to imagine the naval and merchant marine force structure required to satisfy strategic sealift requirements.[199] This official re-commitment to sealift is continued two years later by the Navy in a follow-on White Paper. As "Forward... From the Sea" explains to its readers: "Because we are a maritime nation, our security strategy is necessarily a transoceanic one. Our vital interests—those interests for which the United States is willing to fight—are at the endpoint of the 'highways of the seas' or lines of strategic approach that stretch from the United States to the farthest point on the globe."[200] Whatever else sea power may be evolving into, it is clear that the world's most powerful sea power still considers transportation a vital (if unglamorous) maritime capability that it must posses.

This said, there exists in American policy circles significant debate about how best to fulfil the strategic sealift need. The conventional wisdom has been that America must retain an independent merchant fleet capable of meeting the bulk of American strategic needs during an international conflict. In recent decades this has required government subsidies to privately owned merchant fleets. Despite government financial assistance, the US merchant fleet has shrunk from a high of 3,500 vessels in 1945 to 322 vessels today.[201] The US no longer has a merchant marine capable of independently meeting American strategic needs during a global war. The conventional wisdom that America maintain an independent, domestic-built merchant fleet is not without its detractors. Claiming that they are simply facing the economic realities of the modern shipbuilding industry, these critics recommend that the US purchase the requisite merchant vessels, rather than continuing to subsidize a dying American industry.[202] Though less sound strategically, the detractors' offer of a less expensive alternative to heavy subsidies is meeting with limited approval in some quarters.

The concept that an army 'moves on its belly' is a truism that speaks to the logistical requirements of modern military formations. This factor is no doubt just as important, and perhaps more so, for navies.[203] As Winston Churchill stated, "Victory is the beautiful, bright-colored flower. Transportation is the stem without which it would never bloom."[204] To take positive advantage of sea control a nation must posses the capacity to transport strategically important goods, equipment, and personnel across the oceans. Such capabilities need not be, and likely will not be, completely uncontested by the enemy. Any competent opponent will understand the implications of their opponent having free reign to transport commodities across the oceans—a competent opponent will interfere if he can. Achieving relative control of the sea offers a nation what Gray termed "the leverage of sea power." The resources of the world are made available to the nation possessing positive control of the seas.

## PLANES AND BOATS

In an age of jet aircraft and spaceships it seems somehow archaic to point out that modern transportation internationally, both civil and military, is still principally dependent upon boats plying the world's oceans. Mahan's often cited summation of ocean-borne transport, "Notwithstanding all the familiar and unfamiliar dangers of the sea, both travel and traffic by water have always been easier and cheaper than by land,"[205] seems a quaint lexicon today. So promising appears the future of flight that futurists have predicted the obsolescence of sea-borne methods of transporting goods and commodities for many decades; the assent of the airplane seems always just around the corner. And indeed, it does seem likely that in some distant future aircraft will replace ships as the prime movers of international goods. When considering this potential Brodie suggests that "If in the future the greater part of ocean transport is carried in aircraft rather than in ships, or if the transfer of men and commodities across the seas becomes unimportant, sea power as such will cease to have meaning."[206] The implications of Brodie's words ring loudly as we are informed that the volume of international trade transported by airplane is growing rapidly. Indeed, the declining relevance of merchant vessels to both the global economy and military power projection are cited as reasons that sea power is fading away as an aspect of state power.

Noting the dramatic increase internationally of goods shipped by air, unfortunately, offers a genuinely skewed look at the realities of international trade. One is reminded of the adage that statistics never lie, but liars use statistics. It is true that some high value commodities, like computer chips, can be shipped cost-effectively by air; such high value markets have spearheaded the dramatic increase in dollar value of freight shipped internationally by air. However, the overall volume of international trade

### United States' Exports, by Method of Transport: 1980 to 1994

| Item | Unit | 1980 | 1985 | 1990 | 1993 | 1994 |
|------|------|------|------|------|------|------|
| All methods | Bil. Dol. | 220.7 | 213.1 | 393.0 | 464.9 | 512.4 |
| Vessel | Bil. Dol. | 120.9 | 91.7 | 150.8 | 166.6 | 177.6 |
| Air | Bil. Dol. | 46.1 | 52.3 | 110.5 | 135.1 | 150.3 |
| Shipping weight: Vessel | Bil. Kg. | 363.7 | 317.7 | 372.4 | 349.5 | 334.5 |
| Air | Bil. Kg. | 1.0 | 0.8 | 1.5 | 1.7 | 2 |

*Source:* US Bureau of the Census, *Statistical Abstract of the US: 1995*, page 662. "All methods" category includes transportation types other than vessel and air, and contains table revisions not distributed by method of transport. Units are billions of 1980 US dollars, and billions of kilograms.

conducted by air remains woefully small compared to trade conducted by water. Consider the following table that shows American exports by method of transport over a fourteen year period.

This table shows that the United States, the world leader in avionics, has reached a point where the value of goods exported by air transport now rivals the value exported by vessel. The increased value of American air transported exports over the last fourteen years is remarkable; it is also misleading. As recently as 1994 America shipped abroad a mere 2 billion kilograms of goods by air; this same year America transported 334 billion kilograms of goods by vessel.[207] More importantly, as a percentage of total goods shipped internationally, air transport is still quite small. A handful of technologically capable nations trade high value commodities, like computer chips, that are light enough to make air transport practical. However, most commodities transported by even these nations is still transported by vessel. Other less technologically advanced nations transport almost none of their goods by air.

Where technological advances in aviation are much commented upon, important advances in the design of merchant vessels is rarely given serious thought. Until the success of *guerre de course* campaigns during World War II led to design changes in merchantmen, most merchant vessels fell in the ten to twelve knot speed bracket. With no competition from other forms of transport, the design of merchant vessels had grown stagnant. Where the requirements of war spurred design innovation during the Second World War, economic competition demands innovation in ship designs today. Shippers are currently exploring designs that may increase a merchant ship's speed to sixty knots.[208] Owners and operators of merchant fleets have come to realize that a single 60 knot vessel is worth more than three 20 knot vessels, since 60 knot vessels will go a long way toward diminishing the major advantage currently held by airlines: speed of delivery. So long as merchant vessels remain competitive in delivery dates (that is, they may be slower than aircraft, but not absurdly so) their greatly lower operating costs should ensure their continued domination as carriers of international trade. To truly cut into the percentage of goods transported by merchant vessels, aircraft will have to greatly lower operating costs while simultaneously increasing payload capabilities.

## MERCHANT FLEETS AND FORCE PROJECTION

Beyond protecting economic assets and lifelines, maritime power provides a force projection capability that is a significant aspect of a nation's overall military power. To effectively project military force abroad a nation must be able to transport soldiers, equipment, ammunition, fuel, water, food, and replacements to vital areas in a timely manner. In practice the protection of the nation from overland threats is normally the first military priority. Whether national policy is basically aggressive or defensive in nature, land threats constitute the first level of strategic considerations. Once a nation determines that its land frontiers are safe[209], then sea avenues of approach can be considered. A similar strategic calculus is normally undertaken by aggressive nations; that is, aggressors will first consider invading those nations one's military can reach by land, and then consider those nations reachable by sea. The strategic requirements of force projection are layered and prioritized. Chinese strategists would be foolish to concentrate on developing the capacity to project power into the South China Sea while China's land frontiers went unguarded. The fact that the Chinese are actively developing significant force projections capabilities in the South China Sea suggests that Chinese strategists consider higher strategic priorities to have already been fulfilled.

It is not enough to recognize Napoleon's truism that 'an army marches on its stomach'—like Napoleon, a plan must be crafted to overcome the logistic problems faced by your military. Many of the best known military proverbs are a reflection upon logistics. Whether we consider the standing order of Confederate Lieutenant General Nathan Bedford Forrest to "get there fustest with the mostest," or Marshal Turenne's cynical observation that "God is always on the side of the big battalions," we find military leaders necessarily obsessed with placing men and material in adequate numbers at the decisive location at the decisive time. As a look at a map of the world quickly shows, the ability to project military power across oceans in of essential strategic importance to states with great power aspirations.

Van Creveld calls the problems of logistics "the hardest facts of all" in the military equation; logistics is the issue that comes before any thought of maneuver, penetration, or encirclement.[210] In 1941 the United States had just under 500 large merchant ships in its merchant marine; this number is rather abstract until one considers that during the course of the Second World War some 733 large American merchant ships were sunk.[211] The US merchant fleet grew to over 5,600 ships during the conflict.[212] Browning reminds us that "during the war 203,522,000 tons of dry cargo, 64,730,00 tons of petroleum products, 1,000,000 vehicles, 24,000 aircraft, and over 7,000,000 troops and civilians were carried by American ships."[213] Browning demonstrates that this incredible sealift effort translates to over 8,000 tons of cargo delivered every hour, every day and night, of the entire war. Compare this grand effort to the modest contingencies planned for by today's military leadership. The US Army has recently committed itself to placing a heavy brigade afloat in prepositioned ships.[214] The brigade will be "2x2;" that is, it will consist of the equipment required for two armored battalions and two mechanized infantry battalions. This structure will allow the local commander the flexibility of constructing any of the three heavy brigade composites that currently exist in the US Army: 1) the armor-heavy (2x1) brigade, 2) the mechanized-heavy (1x2) brigade, or 3) the armored cavalry regiment (with fly-in aviation squadron).[215] So committed is the Army to the task of prepositioning equipment afloat that the Marine Corps has become concerned that its unique status as the nation's premier amphibious assault force might be challenged in the near future. The Army's commitment to the development of a 2x2 brigade permanently afloat in prepositioned vessels, with all required equipment and supplies aboard, is a tremendous logistical undertaking. The US Army estimates that 54 M60A3 tanks operating in moderate terrain would consume roughly 15,573.38 gallons of diesel fuel *per day*.[216] These tanks would also be estimated to *individually* consume 55 rounds of ammunition on the first day of a moderate defensive operation, and some 33 rounds on each succeeding day of the defensive operation.[217] Fifty-five rounds of ammunition for a single M60 equates to 1.980 standard tons of transportable supply goods; additionally, the estimated 33 rounds required on succeeding days places a daily burden on the supply chain of 1.188 standard tons per tank being supported. To operate the tanks still need fuel, spare parts, repair facilities, and, obviously, tank crews. Tank crews require food, water, clothing and medical facilities. Such requirements quickly move beyond the capabilities of cargo aircraft. We find that moving a heavy brigade equipped with M60s into a combat theater is a serious undertaking; a logistical undertaking that can not be 'thrown together' at the last moment. Obviously, in addition to problems inherent in any large scale logistical operation, an active enemy must be taken into account—what if one (or more) of the cargo vessels does not make it to the area of operations. Supplies and equipment must be dispersed to avoid the loss of any overly vital ship, and a margin of losses during shipping must be considered.

With all the problems associated with strategic sealift, it is only natural to consider strategic airlift as an alternative. We find that due to its weight, only one M60 can be transported per trip in the US Air Force's most capable cargo plane, the C5 Hercules. Troops, supplies, and other equipment would require additional flights. Such a deployment would necessarily be piecemeal, with handfuls of troops and equipment arriv-

**Ammunition Expenditures per Type Unit per Day in Standard Tons**

| | Defense of Position | | Attack of Position (deliberately organized) | | |
|---|---|---|---|---|---|
| | First Day | Succeeding Days | First Day | Succeeding Days | Protracted Period |
| Infantry Division | 1,896.3 | 1,722.0 | 1,579.6 | 1,350.9 | 864.2 |
| Airborne Division | 1,373.4 | 1,277.9 | 1,180.7 | 1,018.7 | 552.2 |
| Armored Division | 2,432.6 | 1,902.8 | 1,911.5 | 1,424.3 | 1,163.4 |
| Separate Armored Brigade | 485.8 | 404.6 | 375.8 | 300.8 | 265.4 |

*Source:* John Edwards' *Combat Service Support Guide*, 1989, pp. 141–144.

ing in each airlift wave. The tactical situation may not allow for such deployment; small forces with no depth would be tempting targets. As a practical matter, the deployment of heavy forces into combat with their crews and material can only be done by merchant vessel.

Understanding the logistical requirements of force projection, one can see limitations on a state's freedom of action arising when the state lacks effective sealift capabilities.

Contrary to the claims of Douhet and his modern followers, air power can not of itself provide victory. Modern warfare requires joint operations to an historically unprecedented degree. A state aspiring to become a great military power must develop competent force projection capabilities, including force projection over oceans. The American ability to project military power (often decisively) during the twentieth century altered the outcomes of the First and Second World Wars. Used to great effect during the landings at Inchon during the Korean War, the American ability to project military force ashore provides ample lessons to those who are willing to learn. One important lesson of this power projection was that the United States, although the world's premier civil and military air power during and after World War II, still had to depend largely upon sea transport to deliver its combat forces to the theaters of operations as recently as the Gulf War. If great continental powers, like

China, desire an ability to project force globally on the scale that America currently possesses, then their maritime doctrines must change.

## THE DECLINE OF THE AMERICAN MERCHANT MARINE

Given the economic and strategic realities of international trade today, it is troubling that American shipyards are closing and downsizing at such an alarming rate. For example, 1993 only one merchant vessel was under construction at all American private shipyards.[218] Merchant marines provide economic leverage in times of peace, strategic leverage in times of war. Such leverage in war and peace translates into political influence.[219] Yes, the US government can purchase foreign built merchant vessels for less money than it can purchase American built vessels. And yet, if the US government allows American shipyards to wither on the vine, this would represent a serious strategic weakness. It is one thing to purchase merchant vessels during times of peace, who can guarantee continued sales during times of international conflict? Further, a weakened shipbuilding industry will not only be unable to meet national merchant vessel requirements, it also will not be prepared to meet wartime demands for the construction of warships.

As American transport capabilities decline, the transport capabilities of potential adversaries, like China, grows. One must ask, why do the Chinese desire a large merchant marine? China possesses a largely self-sufficient economy and does not engage heavily in international trade (though this is slowly changing). For an island nation like Japan, transportation across the oceans is a requirement—for a continental nation like China, transportation across the oceans is an expensive luxury. A command economy, it is clear that the Chinese investment in an impressive merchant marine is a national priority approved by the highest levels of the Chinese government. It is apparent that the Chinese leadership has a political objective that it feels can be obtained through an application of maritime power. The Chinese decision to first develop a powerful merchant marine, while only slowly developing their naval capabilities, is a politically sound method for developing maritime power. Though merchant marines have significant strategic implications, they are nonetheless easily neglected in the strategic evaluations made by foreign policy makers. It would be more difficult, for example, for American policy makers to neglect the strategic importance of a new Chinese carrier battle group. Thus, the Chinese accomplish two political objectives with their periodic talk of acquiring an aircraft carrier. First, each time the possible acquisition is mentioned, but not moved on, the international community is mentally prepared for the day when China finally does acquire a carrier battle group. When the Chinese finally put their first carrier group to sea the international reaction will likely be: "it had to happen sooner or later, we're lucky it took them this long . . . " Second, as the international community concentrates on a Chinese carrier that has yet to appear, it tends to neglect the general growth and improved capabilities of other Chinese combatants, and the vastly improved capabilities of the Chinese merchant marine.

In 1995, the US Congress voted to extend the Merchant Marine Act.[220] In voicing their support for the proposed legislation, members of the House of Representatives pointed to the fact that 90 percent of logistical supplies in Desert Storm-Desert Shield arrived via sealift.[221] First passed by Congress in 1936, this act serves to bolster domestic production of merchant vessels.[222] The vote over this vital national recourse was highly controversial; a similar bill had been blocked in committee in the Senate in 1994.[223] Such support as there was for the legislation seemed to center on the bill's potential to create jobs, not the bill's ability to provide American policy makers with strategic options during national emergencies. A maritime nation neglects sea transportation capabilities only at its own peril.

## DANGERS OF DEPENDENCE ON FOREIGN SHIPPING

Recognizing the need for shipping in military power projection operations, states like China have embarked on a serious program of developing a large and diversified merchant marine. Such a program is no doubt an expensive, and pointedly non-sexy, strategic commitment for a nation to make. Having made the commitment to sealift, China now is prepared to become a maritime power to be reckoned with. To avoid this great expense, or to spend the national security/military budget on programs that appear more enticing to the public, some nations have determined that their strategic sealift needs will be purchased from allies and neutral nations during times of war.[224] It is reasonable to assume that the merchant marine of an active wartime partner would be made available during a war—dismissing for the moment the issue of whether one's confederate could afford to share this valuable recourse—since the joint use of this resource would favor the war position of the entire alliance. Although problems stemming from national differences in war aims and wartime priorities might cause some concern, it is at least plausible that allied shipping will be available. However, some strategic planners, American officials for example, assume passage on both allied and neutral shipping. The American experience in the Gulf War saw significant use of allied and neutral shipping, thus strengthening the arguments of those claiming that the US does not need a large independent merchant fleet. For others the issue of neutral countries supporting American interests during international conflicts raises serious concern. Machiavelli's warning of the futility of using mercenary and auxiliary forces in *The Prince* may offer a useful moral to modern sea powers. While the notion of a modern state employing mercenary military forces is unrealistic today, the ability to make military use of foreign owned, civilian manned cargo vessels is an increasingly significant aspect of national contingency planning. Machiavelli's warnings have been forgotten.

> Mercenaries and auxiliaries are useless and dangerous. If a prince bases the defence of his state on mercenaries he will never achieve stability or security. For mercenaries are disunited, thirsty for power, undisciplined, and disloyal; they are brave among their friends and cowards before the enemy; they have no fear of God, they do not keep faith with their fellow men; in peacetime you are despoiled by them, and in wartime by the enemy. The reason for all this is that there is no loyalty or inducement to keep them on the field apart from the little they are paid, and this is not enough to make them want to die for you. They are only too ready to serve in your army when you are not at war; but when war comes they either desert or disperse.[225]

Substitute a nation such as America for "a prince," and further think of purchasing cargo space rather than infantry companies, and we are left with a disturbing avenue of logical argument that effectively upends a significant assumption of European and American strategists. Yes, a foreign merchant marine will gladly carry our national freight, for a tidy profit, during times of peace. Obviously the services of this merchant marine will be denied us if we go to war with that nation; conversely, if that nation is an active wartime ally, we should retain some use of these vessels.[226] But, will the foreign merchant marine be willing to put ships and lives in harms way if from a neutral state?[227] Carrying goods for a nation at war, especially the obvious move of carrying actual military equipment and personnel, can be considered an act of war. In effect, Western strategists are assuming that many nations will be willing to risk war. With the case of Iraq during the Gulf War, many nations were willing to risk antagonizing a regional land

## Merchant Vessels, World and United States: 1960 to 1993

| Year | World: Completed | | World: Owned | | US: Completed | | US: Owned | |
|------|--------|-------------------|--------|-------------------|--------|-------------------|--------|-------------------|
| | Number | Gross tonnage | Number | Gross tonnage | Number | Gross tonnage | Number | Gross tonnage |
| 1960 | 2,005 | 8,382 | 36,311 | 129,770 | 49 | 379 | 4,059 | 24,837 |
| 1970 | 2,814 | 20,980 | 52,444 | 227,490 | 156 | 375 | 2,983 | 18,463 |
| 1980 | 2,412 | 13,101 | 73,832 | 419,911 | 205 | 555 | 5,579 | 18,464 |
| 1985 | 1,964 . | 18,157 | 76,395 | 416,369 | 66 | 180 | 6,447 | 19,518 |
| 1990 | 1,672 | 15,885 | 78,336 | 423,627 | 16 | 15 | 6,348 | 21,328 |
| 1991 | 1,574 | 16,095 | 80,030 | 436,027 | 17 | 9 | 6,222 | 20,291 |
| 1992 | 1,506 | 18,633 | 79,845 | 444,305 | 27 | 54 | 5,737 | 18,228 |
| 1993 | 1,505 | 20,025 | 80,655 | 457,915 | 30 | 14 | 5,646 | 14,087 |

*Source:* US Bureau of the Census, *Statistical Abstract of the US: 1995*, page 666. Gross tonnage (1,000). 1993 is most recent year data is tabulated.

power that was about to be destroyed by American military power. It is unfounded to assume that nations will risk warfare with all American adversaries. As nations like the United States continue to lose relative position internationally in merchant vessel tons, two solutions present themselves. First, a nation might develop increased carrying capacity. This solution is expensive, though strategically sound. Second, a nation could create contingency planning which assumes the free use of neutral shipping. This solution is inexpensive, and therefore many will gravitate to it. Strategically the second solution has little merit, but long-term strategic reasoning has often been known to fall in the face of short-term economic gain. Consider the declining state of the American merchant marine in the following table. We find that in 1960 the United States owned just over 11% of all merchant vessels in the world; by 1993 that number had fallen to 7% of the total. Perhaps more telling than number of merchant vessels, the gross tonnage of American merchantmen fell from 19% of the world total in 1960 to 3% of the total in 1993.

The numbers in the above tables are often dismissed for two reasons: first, it is claimed that the United States (or more precisely, its citizens) actually owns many more vessels than this—those vessels are simply flying flags of convenience elsewhere, and second, even accepting that American shipbuilding capacity is falling away, so what? If we

**Merchant Fleets of the World per Registry: 1993**

| Country of Registry/ | Total | Passenger Cargo Comb. | Freighters | Bulk Carriers | Tankers |
|---|---|---|---|---|---|
| 1. Panama | 3,323 | 31 | 1,794 | 745 | 753 |
| 2. Liberia | 1,515 | 29 | 384 | 470 | 632 |
| 3. Russia | 1,443 | 13 | 1,133 | 89 | 208 |
| 4. Cyprus | 1,373 | 13 | 635 | 565 | 160 |
| 5. China | 1,311 | 28 | 788 | 307 | 188 |
| 6. Greece | 970 | 22 | 192 | 483 | 273 |
| 7. Japan | 881 | 16 | 320 | 219 | 326 |
| 8. Bahamas | 863 | 54 | 414 | 155 | 240 |
| 9. Malta | 852 | 6 | 366 | 287 | 193 |
| 10. Norway | 665 | 14 | 199 | 156 | 296 |
| 11. United States | 564 | 12 | 321 | 21 | 210 |
| 12. Singapore | 526 | - | 229 | 93 | 204 |
| 13. Saint Vincent | 524 | 4 | 348 | 100 | 72 |
| 14. Philippines | 522 | 5 | 225 | 244 | 48 |
| 15. Ukraine | 448 | 14 | 348 | 55 | 31 |
| 16. South Korea | 408 | - | 213 | 120 | 75 |
| 17. Germany | 376 | 6 | 308 | 16 | 44 |
| 18. Hong Kong | 214 | - | 68 | 116 | 28 |
| 19. Vanuatu | 122 | - | 58 | 53 | 11 |

*Source:* US Bureau of the Census, *Statistical Abstract of the US: 1995*, page 667.

decide that we need to increase our relative share of world gross tonnage capacity, can't we buy vessels from allies like Japan and South Korea who are major producers? First let us examine the issue of flags of convenience. It is true that nations like Panama and Liberia do not own as many vessels as it appears. Consider the following table which lists, by registry, the major international players.

Listing of merchant marines by country of registry dominate available data sources on merchant marines. The problem with lists by registry is that many vessels are registered with "flag of convenience" nations in

**World Merchant Fleets per Vessel Owner: As of January 1, 1997**
**Top 20 nationalities of parent company (vessel owner)**
**Merchant type vessels 999 gross tons and over.**

| Rank | Number Vessels | Total DWT | Nationality of Parent Company |
|------|---------------|-----------|-------------------------------|
| 1 | 2,849 | 119,712,440 | Greece |
| 2 | 2,587 | 87,838,841 | Japan |
| 3 | 1,817 | 35,904,212 | People's Republic of China |
| 4 | 1,741 | 15,197,962 | Russia |
| 5 | 1,250 | 17,785,765 | Germany |
| 6 | 1,148 | 47,820,095 | Norway |
| 7 | 1,061 | 52,010,508 | United States |
| 8 | 776 | 17,685,220 | Singapore |
| 9 | 728 | 22,856,388 | Republic of South Korea |
| 10 | 666 | 34,811,025 | Hong Kong |
| 11 | 583 | 20,586,791 | United Kingdom |
| 12 | 518 | 10,041,293 | Turkey |
| 13 | 517 | 12,239,050 | Denmark |
| 14 | 516 | 4,234,260 | Indonesia |
| 15 | 491 | 11,339,210 | Italy |
| 16 | 477 | 5,371,118 | Netherlands |
| 17 | 477 | 7,754,232 | Panama |
| 18 | 450 | 4,731,682 | Ukraine |
| 19 | 437 | 14,968,182 | Taiwan |
| 20 | 355 | 12,451,536 | India |
| Subtotal of top 20 | 19,444 | 555,339,810 | |
| | 7,414 | 164,539,085 | all other nations |
| World total | 26,858 | 719,878,895 | |

*Source:* April 11, 1997 letter from Robert L. Brown, Chief, Division of Statistical Analysis, US Maritime Administration. Mr. Brown took his information from the Lloyd's Ship Particulars File as of January 1, 1997.

efforts to skirt taxes and hide ownership. Information more difficult to find, but often more useful, is international shipping rankings based upon national ownership instead of national registry.

As we can see, the above table ranks nations by the number of vessels owned. Another useful ranking is by total deadweight tons (DWT) of the merchant fleet owned. For a presentation of this information ranked by DWT, please see Appendix C.

## IMITATION AS FLATTERY

Successful nations tend to be copied.[228] The United States owes much of its current military potential to its considerable investment in naval power. Nations that wish to contest American policy and military power abroad must first develop a reliable means for getting their military forces into the theatre of operations. Consider the current strategic position of China: For all practical purposes the Chinese can currently use their army, the world's largest, against the United States only if America attempted an invasion of China. That is, American ground forces would have to move to a position in or near China from which the PLA could engage them. Currently, the Chinese military simply lacks the power projection capabilities required for operations outside of mainland East Asia.[229] The Chinese are well aware of this strategic limitation. Why have the Chinese invested so heavily in their merchant marine over the last 25 years? The Chinese economy is not dependent upon foreign trade. A centrally planned economy, it is clear that Chinese entrepreneurs are not responsible for going to sea to seek their fortunes. This investment in sea power is government planned and approved. A serious improvement in naval capabilities would have been limiting unless coupled with the transport capability that the Chinese merchant marine now offers the Chinese government. Diplomatically, it was easy for the Chinese to develop the mercantile half of their sea power component, since transport vessels are generally not feared. More recently, the Chinese, already established as a merchant power, are now developing their naval power. In 1970 the Chinese had 13 destroyers and destroyer escorts. In 1995 the number had risen to 50.[230] By way of comparison, the Japanese had 27 destroyers and destroyer escorts in 1970; in 1995 they had 63. While some may point to the missing Chinese aircraft carrier as the key non-event of vessel acquisition in an Asian naval arms race, it is destroyers that comprise the backbone of a naval force. In terms of ship quality and numbers of vessels, clearly the Chinese are gaining on this important East Asian rival.

**NOTES**

197. Bernard Brodie, *A Layman's Guide to Naval Strategy*, 1942, p. 8.

198. "... From the Sea," p. 3.

199. In the current international system all nations can use sea transport if they can afford to buy space aboard the multinational merchant marine; thus some argue that there is no pressing need in peacetime to own one's own merchant fleet. However, a dependence on foreign owned merchant vessels holds strategic implications should war come—this issue will be explored in more depth later in this chapter.

200. "Forward... From the Sea," p. 2.

201. Information found in Lieutenant Commander Sean T. Connaughton's "Reinventing Sealift," *Proceedings*, December 1997, p. 60.

202. See Connaughton's "Reinventing Sealift," *Proceedings*, December 1997, pp. 59–61, for an example of a critic of continued subsidies for the US shipbuilding industry.

203. Martin Van Creveld's *Supplying War*, Cambridge University Press, 1977, may be useful to readers interested in military logistics. Alfred Thayer Mahan notes that Nelson, in addition to being a great strategist and tactician, was also a great administrator of logistics. Without his logistical talents, Nelson's fighting spirit would have mattered little. Found in *Naval Administration and Warfare*, 1918, p. 320.

204. Found in Thomas Manzagol and Eleni Brown's "Where's My Stuff?," *Army Logistician*, May-June 1996, p. 10.

205. Alfred Thayer Mahan, *Influence of Sea Power*, 1987 edition, p. 25.

206. Bernard Brodie, *A Layman's Guide to Naval Strategy*, 1942, p. 4.

207. Those who note that the volume of US exports shipped by air has doubled in the last fourteen years, while the volume shipped by vessel has remained static, grossly misuse statistics. It is relatively easy to double very small numbers, and the volume of US exports transported by air was a very small number indeed in 1980. Significantly, less than 1% of the volume of American exports move by air.

208. Jacques Bally, "The Shape of Ships to Come II," *Armada International*, February/March 1996, 1/1996E, pp. 6–15.

209. For example, the United States considers its Canadian and Mexican borders to be secure; this could always change if the international situation changes, or if the foreign policy of one of the North American governments significantly changes. England felt its borders secure to the coastline only after Wales and Scotland were incorporated into the United Kingdom. Russia has never considered its borders secure.

210. Martin Van Creveld, *Supplying War*, 1977, p. 1.

211. In *U.S. Merchant Vessel War Casualties of World War II*, Naval Institute Press, 1996, p. xvii, Robert Browning claims that the U.S. Merchant Marine stood at just under 500 vessels on the eve of the war. Others, like John Bunker in *Heroes in Dungarees*, Naval Institute Press, 1995, p. xi, state figures around 1,400 vessels. The discrepancy reflects different methods of vessel classification. For example, Bunker includes in his numbers "a sizable fleet of passenger vessels, mostly in the coastal, intercoastal, and Caribbean trades." Browning does not find it useful to count such vessels since they would not be engaged in global sea-lift. Browning puts American merchant losses at "over 700" while Bunker provides the exact number of 733 on p. xii.

212. Robert Browning, *U.S. Merchant Vessel War Casualties of World War II*, 1996, p. xvii. See *The United States Merchant Marine at War, Report of the War Shipping Administration to the President*, US Printing Office, 1946, for detailed information regarding American merchant marine during the Second World War. This source was found in Browning's book.

213. Robert Browning, *U.S. Merchant Vessel War Casualties of World War II*, 1996, p. xvii.

214. See James Pasquarette and William Foster, "An Army Heavy Brigade Goes Afloat," *Naval Institute Proceedings*, May 1994, pp. 89–92.

215. James Pasquarette and William Foster, "An Army Heavy Brigade Goes Afloat," *Naval Institute Proceedings*, May 1994, p. 91.

216. John Edwards, *Combat Service Support Guide*, Stackpole Books, 1989, p. 81. Edwards, a major in the US Army, bases his calculations upon readings of US Army Field Manuals.

217. Edwards shows that a heavy defensive would require 78 rounds, while a light defensive is estimated to require 34 rounds (p. 151). Offensive operations are estimated to require fewer rounds: heavy attack 65 rounds the first day, moderate attack 46 rounds the first day, light attack 28 rounds the first day.

218. Page 664–5 in the US Bureau of the Census, *Statistical Abstract of the US: 1995*, shows declining employment and construction at US shipyards from 1980 through 1993. Were it not for the construction of naval vessels, purposefully ordered and delivered to provide constant work to the shipyards, the US shipbuilding industry would surely collapse.

219. See Laurence Martin's *The Sea in Modern Strategy*, Frederick A. Praeger Publishers, 1967, p. 17, for a discussion of the political importance of the Soviet Union's growing merchant marine fleet during the Cold Wars years.

220. *Congressional Quarterly Almanac*, 104th Congress, 1st Session, 1995, Volume LI, pp. 3–70 to 3–71.

221. Mr. Livingston, *Congressional Record*, Wednesday, December 6, 1995, Volume 141, Number 193, p. H 14061.

222. For an explanation of current legislation's ties to the original 1936 legislation, please see Mr. Quillen's comments, *Congressional Record*, Tuesday, August 2, 1994, Volume 140, Number 104, p. H 6567. Mr. Quillen suggests that the original act was passed "during a period of relative tranquillity" because Congress correctly understood that the American maritime industry was close to dying. Congress understood then that the United States would need this industry in times of crisis. While one can grasp the strategic logic of a maritime nation maintaining a viable maritime industry, today or in 1936, one does question the attempt to label 1936 a tranquil year.

223. See *Congressional Quarterly Almanac*, 104th Congress, 1st Session, 1995, Volume LI, pp. 3–70 to 3–71 and *Congressional Quarterly Almanac*, 103rd Congress, 2nd Session, 1994, Volume L, pp. 158–160.

224. Consider the problems faced by American planners when crews of merchant vessels refused to take their ships into harm's way during the recent Gulf War. Eventually these vessels were taken over and manned by US Navy sailors. In this case, the cargo did arrive. Still, the precedent does not bode well for future operations dependent upon foreign civilian cargo shipping.

225. Niccolo Machiavelli, *The Prince*, Penguin Books, 1961 edition, pp. 77–78.

226. Even allied nations may have some trouble continuing wartime support of their merchant marines. During the Gulf War the United States Navy was forced to take over a German merchant ship, loaded with US Army tanks, when the ship's captain refused to sail into the Gulf. US Navy crews had to sail the final leg of the trip to Saudi Arabia. Though Germany was an ally during the Gulf War, the German civilian sailors aboard that merchantman felt no obligation to sail into harm's way.

227. The US Congress addressed this issue in 1995 when debating the proposed Merchant Marine Act. As stated on the floor of the House of Representatives: "In times of crisis, we cannot depend on foreign ships and foreign crews for sealift and sustainment requirements. Why should we rely on Third World crew who have no allegiance to the U.S. to deliver equipment, medical supplies, and materials that American service men and women need as they fight to protect America's interest abroad? We should not and we cannot." Found in *Congressional Record*, Wednesday, December 6, 1995, Volume 141, Number 193, p. H 14061.

228. In *Theory of International Politics*, McGraw-Hill, 1979, Kenneth Waltz claims that nations will either emulate other nations that are relatively successful "or fall by the wayside" (118). Waltz is suggesting that much as an individual can tailor his activities after someone he respects as successful, so to can

governments learn to be successful by observing the activities and past decisions that successful nations have made.

229. "Beijing to Build More Ports With Foreign Capital." Washington DC, *FBIS-CHI-94–236*, December 7, 1994, p. 27.

230. *The Military Balance*, 1970, pp. 58 and 64. *The Military Balance*, 1995, pp. 177 and 182.

# CHAPTER 4

# Sea Power in the 21st Century

> *No valid conception of sea power can vary*
> *according to the psychology or culture of differ-*
> *ent nations. A concept of sea power is either*
> *correct and conforms with the realities of war,*
> *or it is wrong.*[231]
>
> —BERNARD BRODIE

## SEA POWER IN THE 21ST CENTURY

This paper has suggested that the character and application of sea power will change in the next century due to transformations in technological innovation and national economic dependence upon the sea. Organizational responses to technological innovation will prove decisive in sustaining modern armed forces. In summary, organizational responses to technological innovation varies; organizational responses to technological innovation matters.

Various interconnected phenomena, including an advanced rate of technological advancement, the changed international system, and the evolving international economic system, together have the capability of greatly impacting the development and sustainment of sea power in the twenty-first century. The synergy created by these phenomena, with the advanced rate of technological innovation acting as the driving force, has the potential to remake the character of sea power. New national capabilities combined with material needs and the evolving strategic environment suggest that the character of sea power may move ever closer to that of land power in the next century. The point is not that the exercise of sea power will become indistinguishable from land power, though this may well occur. Due to advances in technology, it seems likely that the traditional operational and tactical problems associated with land power will now increasingly be seen at sea. The implications of this change, should it in fact occur, will be tremendous. Geopolitics as we now understand it would be changed forever. Man will certainly continue to estab-

lish his presence at sea in ever more permanent ways. As this presence
increases, the most obvious example of a serious change in geopolitics is
the possibility that "freedom of the sea" will lose its meaning. If, or perhaps when, nations exert territorial claims over regions of the oceans, the
impact on international politics will be great. The regions of the oceans
containing the wealthiest natural resource deposits are already becoming
strategically important to nations; it is not difficult to imagine states willing to fight over the control of such regions. Advances in science and
technology is the key to understanding sea power in the next century. All
maritime states will seek to outdo one another in the development of relevant technology; importantly, history suggests that nations can direct
such scientific and technological discovery.

In international politics traditions of success count for a great deal;
in addition to the direct fruits of victory, past success offers the perception of current strength. As Bernard Brodie states

> In the politics of power, military prestige is the medium of account,
> and nothing gives a nation greater prestige than past military victories.
> The political, economic, and most of all technological conditions
> under which those victories were won may have changed, but this
> counts for little except among the most discerning few. Foreign policy
> tends to run along channels determined by tradition, and Powers which
> have been great are considered great until they are proved otherwise.[232]

Brodie's observation appears apt; most scholars and military professionals consider the United States to be the world's premier naval power,
though it has been decades since America has had to fight a major naval
battle. However, past success is not without its own unwanted baggage.
In "Forward. . . From the Sea" the US Navy hierarchy claims that the
fleet's basic building blocks will remain Aircraft Carrier Battle Groups
and Amphibious Ready Groups in the foreseeable future.[233] These naval
formations are highly flexible and have served the fleet well in the past.
Whether they will serve the fleet as well in future combat is an open
question.

Other nations may simply recognize American areas of superiority
in conventional naval warfare and opt to contest a political issue at sea by
using a different paradigm. As Bacevich reminds us

> Like the German navy of the First World War—stymied by British su-
> periority in dreadnoughts—those disadvantaged by the existing rules

will devise new rules more amenable to their interests. Thus, while Americans dazzle themselves with the latest military application of advanced technologies, America's challengers will seek ways of rendering that technology superfluous.[234]

Bacevich's point is that unable to compete dreadnought to dreadnought in a naval arms race, the German Navy competed quite superbly with an unconventional weapon, the submarine. This new vessel would in fact revolutionize naval warfare to a far greater extent than did the *Dreadnought* herself.[235]

Rasler and Thompson suggest that conventional sea powers historically face a complicated decline in relative national power.

> Because their rise is predicated in part on some innovation advantages, their relative decline hinges, to a large degree, on the loss of these advantages. The basic pattern is one of innovation waves. For a period of time, the global leaders possess a virtual monopoly in the control of either critical markets or the production of significant commodities. Each innovation era plays itself out.[236]

And, even if the current wave of innovation is still dominant, a nation recognizing the technological superiority of American military power may chose to contest an issue with other than conventional military forces. Terrorist attacks, tacitly supported acts of piracy, and other low scale operations may be employed by an enemy to gain a political victory in those scenarios where a military victory over the United States seems unlikely.[237] America may find itself proudly fielding the most potent military force that the world has ever seen, only to discover that finding our enemy is impossible. And all the while, the true importance of sea power—transportation, not warships—may be in jeopardy. In "America's Information Edge," Nye and Owens suggest that the United States enjoys a position of leadership in information technology that should last into the foreseeable future.[238] As stated throughout this paper, such a sentiment can lead to a sense of complacency that is dangerous. It is all too easy to treat America's current technological lead as a permanent fixture of international relations instead of treating it as a transitory condition that the United States must endeavor to retain. Perhaps just as dangerous is the tendency to view warfare as an increasingly antiseptic affair. The growing tendency of scholars and political commentators, and indeed, even of military personnel, to contemplate warfare as something other than the use of force to impart the fear of violent death is an invitation to a very rude awakening. In noting the true nature of warfare, Cohen observes that "fear of violent death only comes from the imminent possibility of the real thing."[239]

## TECHNOLOGY'S TWO-WAY STREET

Even if this paper is correct in predicting that an exponentially increased rate of technological innovation will become a dominate characteristic of world power politics generally, and of sea power specifically, it must be pointed out that technological advances tend to act as a two-way street. As America grows dependent upon high technology to solve its problems, is it forgetting numerous low technology solutions to its problems? Worse still, might other nations recognize such solutions?

The United States suffered amazingly light casualties in the recent Gulf War. Technological supremacy over the Iraqi military has widely been credited with this saving of American lives. The United States may not enjoy such an overwhelming technological advantage in its next war; America may find itself roughly equal, or even inferior, to an opponent's military technology. In such a scenario victory will have to be purchased the old fashioned way, with blood, treasure, and tears. Is the nation still up to such a test? A healthy respect for high technology weapons systems will never be able to replace the desire to win. Thus the North Vietnamese could defeat an enemy superior in every conceivable technological criteria. The North Vietnamese will to win guided that people through terrible sacrifices, sacrifices almost inconceivable to their American enemy. Today Americans have almost mythologized the North Vietnamese—we have chosen to remember them as an unbeatable people.[240] We would do better to think of the North Vietnamese not as supermen, but as men willing to endure great sacrifice for a political ideal.

Even small advantages can reap great rewards during international conflict. In 1942 an American naval officer's chance personal knowledge that Midway Island often had fresh water problems led to the breaking of an important Japanese Imperial Navy code. This code breaking set into motion a chain of events, which culminated in a span of fifteen minutes that may well have sealed Japan's fate in the Pacific War. At 10:25 on the morning of June 5, 1942, the Japanese Imperial Navy was at its high water march in the Pacific War, prepared to engage the weaker the US Pacific Fleet in what it hoped would be a decisive naval action. By 10:40 three large Japanese aircraft carriers were sunk—a fourth large Japanese carrier would be lost later in the day. The Japanese Navy would never recover from the loss of these fine vessels or their valuable crews.[241] Many might have difficulty accepting that fifteen minutes of good luck could turn the course of a major war fought between great nations. Such an admission acknowledges the arbitrariness of combat. Yet, fifteen minutes did seal Japan's fate as a maritime power. None can know if a future battle of significance will be decided by a new weapon, or perhaps once again be decided by the seemingly unimportant geographic facts remembered by a mid-level intelligence officer. This research simply makes the point that an emerging technology could provide a nation with their own "fifteen minutes" of good fortune.

## PROVING THE FUTURE

No doubt there will be those who are troubled by the implications of the conclusions this paper has asserted. After all, to suggest a trend that may see the international covenant of freedom of the seas die is no light suggestion. While these ideas are interesting to contemplate, some may ask where the proof is that any of what is suggested will in fact happen. To such criticism I can only state that I have no crystal ball from which to see the future. I have examined trends that many intelligent people have agreed are occurring, though there is still ample debate concerning these trends. I have further examined the significance of those trends with regard to future applications of sea power. Others may find different trends more important or more interesting to reflect upon; for myself, the issues considered in this paper appear to be the key to the future of maritime power.

## NOTES

231. Bernard Brodie's quote was found in Geoffrey Till's *Maritime Strategy and the Nuclear Age*, 1984, p. 11.

232. Bernard Brodie, *Sea Power in the Machine Age*, 1941, p. 434.

233. "Forward. . . From the Sea," p. 4.

234. A. J. Bacevich, "Morality and High Technology," *The National Interest*, Fall 1996, p. 44.

235. It is well known that the original *Dreadnought* represented a huge technological innovation in naval warfare; an innovation that rendered all existing battleships—including British ships—obsolete. However, A. J. Bacevich argues convincingly that the *Dreadnought* in fact reinforced the naval orthodoxy of the day. As he states, ". . . although marking an impressive advance in naval technology, *Dreadnought* served primarily to affirm rather than to subvert the accepted rules of the game" (40).

236. Karen Rasler and William Thompson, "Technological Innovation," *The Journal of Conflict Resolution*, September 1991, p. 419.

237. The fact that naval leaders are concerned with unconventional uses of maritime power is captured nicely in an article appearing in the November 1995 issue of *Naval Proceedings*. "Dragons and Centipedes at Sea" relays an account of a war in the South China Sea between the United States and China in the year 2006. American forces win a costly military victory only to lose the political battle. During this hypothetical war American forces were frustrated by Chinese military and para-military units that played by a vastly different set of rules.

238. Joseph Nye and William Owens, "America's Information Edge," *Foreign Affairs*, March/April 1996, p. 20.

239. Eliot Cohen, "The Mystique of U.S. Air Power," *Foreign Affairs*, January/February 1994, p. 122.

240. In World War II the United States fought two adversaries, Germany and Japan, who had almost fanatically motivated personnel in their militaries. Yet, our answer to fascism and totalitarianism was to steady ourselves to the difficult task at hand. No one suggested, for example, that the Japanese army was unbeatable simply because its troops could be expected to fight well and rarely surrender. To beat the Germans or Japanese we had simply to kill them; somehow this simple truth of war was lost in jungles of Vietnam.

241. Edwin P. Hoyt presents an excellent review of these aspects of the Battle of Midway in *Japan's War: The Great Pacific Conflict*, 1986, pp. 287–299.

# Appendix A

The National Research Council conducted a study for the US Army to determine which emerging technologies were likely to prove important to national security. The committee charged with this task generated a paper titled: *Strategic Technologies for the Army of the Twenty-first Century* (or STAR 21). The following table is taken from their report.

### Army Technology Base Key Emerging Technologies

| Key Emerging Technology | Technology Areas (Selected) | Relevant STAR TFA or Section | STAR High-Payoff Technologies |
|---|---|---|---|
| 1. Advanced Materials and Materials Processing | Composite armor; structural composites; high-temperature engine components; soldier body armor | Advance Materials | material formulation techniques for "designer" materials |
| 2. Microelectronics, Photonics, and Acoustics | VHSIC silicon devices; MMICs; compound semi-conductors; photonic devices; fiber-optic sensors; multispectral sensors; focal plane arrays; infrared sensors | Electronics and Sensors; Optics, Photonics, and Directed Energy | multidomain smart sensors; terahertz-device electronics; secure, wideband communications technology |

| | | | |
|---|---|---|---|
| 3. Advanced Signal Processing and Computing | Software producibility & life cycle; data base management systems; parallel systems; algorithms; automated systems (voice recognition) | Computer Science, Artificial Intelligence, and Robotics | methods & techniques for integrated systems design; battle management software technology |
| 4. Artificial Intelligence | High-speed computation; knowledge acquisition & learning; neural nets; multi sensor data fusion; adaptive control & robotics; AI for logistics, planning, simulation, maintenance, language training | Computer Science, Artificial Intelligence, and Robotics; Electronics and Sensors; Optics, Photonics, Directed Energy | terahertz-device electronics; battle management software technology |
| 5. Robotics | sensors; unmanned ground vehicles; data rate reduction; environmental perception; robot manipulators; various robotics applications | Computer Science, Artificial Intelligence, and Robotics; Electronics and Sensors | |
| 6. Advanced Propulsion Technology | small turbine IHPTET engine cores; VTOL aircraft; ground vehicle transmissions; weapon chemical propulsion | Propulsion and Power | electric-drive technology |
| 7. Power Generation, Storage, and Conditioning | energy storage for pulse power; electric drive power conditioning; fuel cells | Propulsion and Power | |
| 8. Directed Energy | laser efficiency; high energy-density capacitors; switches; high-power microwave | Propulsion and Power | solid state lasers pumped by diode lasers |
| 9. Biotechnology | biosensors and enzyme decontamination for CTBW; vaccines; artificial tissues; multivalent assays for disease; bioremediation; food preservation and packing | Biotechnology and Biochemistry | genetically engineered and developed materials and molecules |

| | | | |
|---|---|---|---|
| 10. Space Technology | communications (man-portable, LIGHTSAT); RISTA; terrain & weather; position & navigation; computation for space systems; fire support | Electronics and Sensors; Environ-mental & Atmos-pheric Sciences; Optics, Photonics, and Directed Energy | methods & tech-niques for inte-grated systems design |
| 11. Low-Observable Technology | radar: absorbing materials and cross-section reduction; infrared: special coatings, vehicle cooling techniques; visual: coatings to suppress or vary reflectance; noise suppression | Electronic and Sensors Advanced Materials | terahertz-device electronics; material formulations for "designer" materials; methods & techniques for integrated systems design |
| 12. Protection and Lethality | armor; soldier eye protec-tion; kinetic energy projec-tiles; explosives; mine detection; CTBW detection, protection, decontamination | Advanced Materials; Propulsion and Power; Biotechnology | material formula-tion techniques for "designer" materi-als; genetically engineered and developed materials and molecules |
| 13. Neuroscience Technology | sleep studies; physiological response to adverse environ-ments; sensory-motor integration applications to advanced weapons systems, robotics | See systems Panel Reports on Health and Medicine; Personnel; Special Technologies | |

*Source: STAR 21*, pp. 272–274.

## NOTES ON ABBREVIATIONS USED IN TABLE:

CTBW refers to Chemical, toxin, or biological warfare.

IHPTET refers to Integrated High-Performance Turbine Engine Technology (an engine research program).

MMIC refers to Monolithic microwave integrated circuit.

RISTA refers to Reconnaissance, intelligence, surveillance, and target acquisition.

TFA refers to Technology Forecast Assessment.

VTOL refers to Vertical takeoff and landing.

# Appendix B

The following Strategic Planning Document is a list of emerging technologies that the United States government asserts have the potential to be decisive. Of course, within the government's various departments there is debate as to which technologies such lists should highlight.

This list was prepared by the Committee for National Security, which advises and assists the National Science and Technology Council (NSTC). The NSTC was established November 23, 1993, as a cabinet-level council to the President in areas of science, space, and technology policies across the Federal government. The NSTC is a part of the Office of Science and Technology Policy (OSTP), which gives expert advice directly to the President in all areas of science and technology. The OSTP is led by a Director and four Associate Directors, all of whom are Presidential appointed and Senate confirmed.

The Committee for National Security advises that the following is not an exhaustive list of Supporting Technologies, and that the list is not presented in any order of importance.

## SAMPLE SUPPORTING TECHNOLOGIES REVIEWED IN SCIENCE AND TECHNOLOGY PROGRAM AREAS

### S&T PROGRAM AREA and SUPPORTING TECHNOLOGIES

#### Aerial Measuring

System Long endurance uavs

Multispectral photography

Geometric correction systems
Radiation dispersal simulators
Differential global positioning
High-purity germanium detector arrays

## Air/Space Vehicles

Astronics
Thermal management
Long endurance uav
Stealthy helicopter insertion
Aerospace propulsion and power
Guidance, navigation and control

## Atmospheric Release Advisory Capability

Database and computer technology

## Battlespace Environments

Weather decision aids
Digital mapping technology
Atmospheric, oceanic and terrain simulation

## Biomedical

Robotics
BW vaccines
Advanced medical treatment
Biological agent neutralization
BW protection equipment (low cost, lightweight)
Special operations forces combat medical support
Neutralization techniques for bw facilities with minimum collateral
damage

## Chemical and Biological Defense

Robotics
Decontamination Information processing and dissemination
Chemical agent detection and neutralization

Low cost, light weight cw equipment technology

Large scale decontamination techniques with minimum collateral damage

Neutralization techniques for chemical warfare facilities

## Civil Engineering

Airfields and pavements

Lightweight superstructures

Critical airbase facilities/recovery

Quick response of airlift and sea lift

Ocean and waterfront facilities/operations

Approaches for temporary shelter/infrastructure

Techniques to support port, airfield, and infrastructure construction in remote locations

Flexible transportation and logistics support planning techniques

Water purification/supply, food distribution, preservation and waste management

Approaches for remote/standoff maintenance and logistics

## Clothing, Textiles and Food

Protective materials

Improved food technologies

Water supply and purification

Food distribution and preservation technologies

Personnel protection from ballistic and laser threats

## Command, Control, Communications (C3) and Intelligence

Moving target indicator

Suppression of enemy C3I

Deployable C3I equipment

Near real-time intelligence

In-transit visibility systems

Signal intelligence technology

Human intelligence technology

Advanced mission planning tools

Automatic decision analysis tools

Real-time data fusion/integration

Improved status monitoring techniques

Non-cooperative combat identification

Improved status monitoring techniques

Military/political intentions intelligence

Local communications traffic monitoring

Rapidly deployable global communications

Automated critical path/node analysis tools

Data collection, fusion, analysis, dissemination

Advanced individual communications techniques

Nuclear safeguards information management system

Atr and automated handling of massive data streams

Information and exchange media (communications and broadcast) for democracy building

Pre-mission intelligence sensing of infrastructure and military/political intentions

Real-time, accurate battle damage assessment algorithms

Global telecommunications and networking to facilitate collection, fusion and analysis

Techniques to facilitate improved intelligence capabilities

Low probability of detection/multi-mode communications for special operations forces

Geographic information systems and advanced mapping tools

**Computers and Software**

Autonomous control logic

Advanced software technologies

Advanced computing architectures

Heterogeneous database integration

Human computer interaction technology

Integration and assessment of information

Compilations and interpretation technologies

Rapid creation and updating of heterogeneous data bases

**Conventional Arms Control**

Non lethal weapons

**Conventional Weapons**

Demining

Electronics

Simulations

Energetic materials

Fuzing technologies

Mine neutralization

Enhanced penetration

Warhead technologies

Minefield marking techniques

Ultra-precision weapon guidance

Specialty munition/weapon techniques

Counter-barrier/mine breeching techniques

Human vulnerability/degradation assessments

Kill mechanisms/lethality (bulk and submunition)

**Directed Energy Weapons**

Particle beam technology

Laser frequency agility technology

Acoustic and electromagnetic technology

**Electronics**

Electro-optics technology

RF components

Microelectronics technology

Electronic materials

Microwave and millimeterwave power modules

**Electronic Warfare**

Camouflage, cover, and deception

Weapon system signature technology

Jamming technologies

Microwave technology

**Environmental Quality**

Modeling and simulation

Transition technologies

Remediation technologies

Alternative energy sources

Advanced sensor technology

Data collection and analysis

Pollution control technologies

**Ground Vehicles**

Robotics

Energy management

Virtual prototyping

Light vehicle protection

Advanced lightweight materials

Signature reduction technologies

**Human Systems Interface**

Performance aiding technology

Crew systems integration and protection

Information management and display technology

**Manpower, Personnel and Training**

Artificial intelligence

Training systems technology

Information storage and retrieval technology

Immersion technologies for remote virtual classrooms

**Manufacturing Science & Technology**

Modeling and simulation

Processing and fabrication technologies

Manufacturing technologies for composites

**Materials, Processes & Structures**

Structural materials

Reliability processing

Design methodologies

Polymeric and composite materials

**Modeling and Simulation**

Architectures

Predictive models

Database integration

Engagement modeling

Environmental modeling

Gaming and predictive database

Real time and historic databases

Advanced distributive simulation

Integrated testbeds and advanced concept technology

**Nuclear Defense**

Hit-to-kill lethality

Hypersonic weapons

Render safe techniques

Advanced TMD concepts

Boost phase intercept concepts

Buried/hard target kill concepts

Advanced kinetic earth penetrators

Nonlethal disabling and isolation techniques

**Nuclear Emergency Search Team**

Containment device

Radiation detectors
Search instrumentation
Ground positioning systems
High-velocity shape charges
Mercuric iodide mini-spectrometers

**Nuclear Stockpile Stewardship**
Electronics
Nuclear materials
Physics of complex systems
High performance computing
Manufacturing technologies
Laser and pulse-power technology
Dynamic testing of complex systems
Chemistry and materials technology
Simulation and modeling of complex systems

**Sensors**
Microsensors
Chemical sensors
Radiation sensing
Radar technology
Lidar/laser radar
X-ray technologies
Imagery generation
Radiation detectors
Multi sensor imaging
Multi-spectral sensors
Counter-sniper sensing
Infrared sensors/imaging
Unattended ground sensors
Automatic target recognition
Detection of crowd formation

Ocean and environment sensors

Counter artillery/mortar sensing

Electro-optic technology/imaging

Tags (material and item) technology

Low cost and man-portable sensors

Remote chemical/biological sensors

Advanced sensor packages (UAV, UGS)

Measurements and signatures technology

Techniques for locating weapons caches

Techniques for locating missing personnel

Near real-time sensing in urban environments

Advanced synthetic aperture radar/radar imaging

Night vision sensors not degraded by illumination

Environmental monitoring sensors (treaty verification)

Robotic sensors and techniques for use in hazardous operations

Wide area, stand-off mine/booby-trap detection

Sensors capable of seeing through walls and/or around corners

Techniques for near real time, wide area surveillance of specific regions

Techniques for monitoring movement of weapons, goods, people

Remotely emplaced, remotely operated, rapidly deployable ground sensors

Techniques for detection of tunnels/caves and underground structures

## Solving Global Problems

Fuel technologies

Waste management

Water supply & purification technologies

Waste & toxic materials control technology

## Special Applications

Classified operational program

### Surface/Undersurface Vehicles

Signal processing

Propulsory technology

Sonar/radar technology

Navigation technologies

Signature reduction technologies

Technology to improve survivability

Shallow water craft technologies and quiet waterjet propulsion

### Technology Cooperation with Former Adversaries/ Industrial Partnering

Safety, security and dismantlement S&T

Cooperative international non-defense related S&T

### Other S&T (e.g., Less-than-lethal programs)

Obscurants

Effective crowd control techniques

Improved psychological operations capability

Techniques for disruption of public infrastructure

Aids in crisis anticipation, prevention and management

Techniques to facilitate expanded use of civil affairs and enhanced civil assessment capability

Techniques for disabling or stopping vehicles in operation

Found at: "http://www.whitehouse.gov/WH/EOP/OSTP/NSTC/html/ns/ ns-apa.html," a White House Internet Site, February 27, 1997.

# Appendix C

World Merchant Fleets as of January 1, 1997
Top 20 nationalities of parent company (vessel owner).
Merchant type vessels 999 gross tons and over.

| Rank by DWT (Rank by No. Vessels) | Number Vessels | Total DWT | Nationality of Parent Company |
|---|---|---|---|
| 1 (1) | 2,849 | 119,712,440 | Greece |
| 2 (2) | 2,587 | 87,838,841 | Japan |
| 3 (7) | 1,061 | 52,010,508 | United States |
| 4 (6) | 1,148 | 47,820,095 | Norway |
| 5 (3) | 1,817 | 35,904,212 | People's Republic of China |
| 6 (10) | 666 | 34,811,025 | Hong Kong |
| 7 (9) | 728 | 22,856,388 | Republic of South Korea |
| 8 (11) | 583 | 20,586,791 | United Kingdom |
| 9 (5) | 1,250 | 17,785,765 | Germany |
| 10 (8) | 776 | 17,685,220 | Singapore |
| 11 (4) | 1,741 | 15,197,962 | Russia |
| 12 (19) | 437 | 14,968,182 | Taiwan |
| 13 (20) | 355 | 12,451,536 | India |

| Rank by DWT (Rank by No. Vessels) | Number Vessels | Total DWT | Nationality of Parent Company |
|---|---|---|---|
| 14 (13) | 517 | 12,239,050 | Denmark |
| 15 (12) | 518 | 10,041,293 | Turkey |
| 16 (15) | 491 | 11,339,210 | Italy |
| 17 (17) | 477 | 7,754,232 | Panama |
| 18 (16) | 477 | 5,371,118 | Netherlands |
| 19 (18) | 450 | 4,731,682 | Ukraine |
| 20 (14) | 516 | 4,234,260 | Indonesia |
| Subtotal of top 20 | 19,444 | 555,339,810 | |
| | 7,414 | 164,539,085 | all other nations |
| World total | 26,858 | 719,878,895 | |

*Source:* April 11, 1997 letter from Robert L. Brown, Chief, Division of Statistical Analysis, US Maritime Administration. Mr. Brown took his information from the Lloyd's Ship Particulars File as of January 1, 1997.

# Works Cited

Adcock, F. E. *The Greek and Macedonian Art of War*. University of California Press; Berkeley, Los Angeles, London. 1957.

Amsden, Alice H. *Asia's Next Giant: South Korea and Late Industrialization*. Oxford University Press; New York and Oxford. 1989.

Angell, Sir Norman. *The Great Illusion: A Study of the Relation of Military Power in Nations to Their Economic and Social Advantage*. G.P. Putnam; New York. 1910.

Angelucci, Enzo and Paolo Matticardi. *Complete Book of World War II Combat Aircraft: 1933–1945*. Military Press; New York. 1988.

Army Institute for Professional Development: Army Correspondence Course Program, Subcourse IT 0469, "US Army Doctrine, Combat Units, and MI Organizations."

Aron, Raymond. *Peace and War: A Theory of International Relations*. Doubleday; new York. 1966.

Auster, Bruce B. "The high-tech cavalry: The Pentagon is betting that new weapons will offset smaller forces." *U.S. News & World Report*. June 28, 1993, p. 29.

*Aviation in the United States Navy*, Naval History Division publication, U.S. Government Printing Office, 1965, p. 1.

Bacevich, A. J. "Morality and High Technology." *The National Interest*. Fall 1996, p. 37.

Bailey, Thomas C. "Application of X-band Radar to Sense Hydrocarbon Seepage," *Oil & Gas Journal*, December 9, 1997, pp. 72–74.

Bally, Captain (Ret.) Jacques J. "The Shape of Ships to Come II." *Armada International*. February/March 1996, 1/1996E, pp. 6–15.

"Beijing to Build More Ports With Foreign Capital." Washington DC, *FBIS-CHI-94–236*, December 7, 1994, p. 27.

Betts, Richard K. *Cruise Missiles: Technology, Strategy, Politics*. The Brookings Institution; Washington, DC 1981.

Blechman, Barry M. and Robert P. Berman. *A Guide to Far Eastern Navies*. Naval Institute Press; Annapolis, Maryland. 1978.

Bradley, David. *No Place to Hide: 1946/1984*. University Press of New England; Hanover and London. 1983 (first published in 1946).

Brodie, Bernard. *A Layman's Guide to Naval Strategy*. Princeton University Press; Princeton, New Jersey. 1942.

Brodie, Bernard. *Sea Power in the Machine Age*. Princeton University Press; Princeton, New Jersey. 1941.

Brodie, Bernard. *Strategy in the Missile Age*. Princeton University Press; Princeton, New Jersey. 1959.

Bronowski, J. *Science and Human Values*. Harper and Row, Publishers; New York. 1965 (first published 1956).

Brown, Robert L. Brown. April 11, 1997 information letter. Mr. Brown is Chief, Division of Statistical Analysis, U.S. Maritime Administration. Mr. Brown took his information from the Lloyd's Ship Particulars File as of January 1, 1997.

Browning, Robert M. Jr. *U.S. Merchant Vessel War Casualties of World War II*. Naval Institute Press; Annapolis, Maryland. 1996.

Bunker, John. *Heroes in Dungarees: The Story of the American Merchant Marine in World War II*. Naval Institute Press; Annapolis, Maryland. 1995.

Callo, Rear Admiral Joseph F. "Finding Doctrine's Future In the Past." *Naval Institute Proceedings*. October 1996, pp. 64–66.

Carr, Edward Hallett. *The Twenty Years' Crisis: 1919–1939*. Harper Books; New York. 1964.

Chernoff, Fred. *After Bipolarity: The Vanishing Threat, Theories of Cooperation, and the Future of the Atlantic Alliance*. The University of Michigan Press; Ann Arbor. 1995.

Claude, Inis. *Power in International Relations*. Random House; New York. 1962.

Clausewitz, Carl von. *On War*. Penguin Books; London. 1982.

Cohen, Eliot A. "The Mystique of U.S. Air Power." *Foreign Affairs*. Vol 73, no 1, January/February 1994, pp. 109–24.

*Combat Fleets of the World: Their Ships, Aircraft, and Armament*. Edited by Bernard Prezelin (with English Language Edition Prepared by A. D. Baker III). Naval Institute Press; Annapolis. 1993.

Connaughton, Lieutenant Commander Sean T. "Reinventing Sealift," *Naval Institute Proceedings*, December 1997, pp 59–61.

Connery, Robert H. *The Navy and the Industrial Mobilization in World War II.* Da Capo Press; New York. 1972.

*Congressional Quarterly Almanac.* Congressional Quarterly Inc; Washington. 104th Congress, 1st Session, 1995, Volume LI.

*Congressional Quarterly Almanac.* Congressional Quarterly Inc; Washington. 103rd Congress, 2nd Session, 1994, Volume L.

*Congressional Record.* United States Government Printing Office; Washington. Tuesday, August 2, 1994, Volume 140, Number 104.

*Congressional Record.* United States Government Printing Office; Washington. Wednesday, December 6, 1995, Volume 141, Number 193.

Crowl, Philip A. "Alfred Thayer Mahan: The Naval Historian." Found in *Makers of Modern Strategy From Machiavelli to the Nuclear Age*, 1986, Peter Paret, editor. Princeton University Press; Princeton, New Jersey. 1986.

Crowther, J. G. and R. Whiddington. *Science at War.* Philosophical Library, Inc.; New York. 1948.

Dandeker, C. "The Bureaucratization of Force." In *War*, Lawrence Freedman, editor. Oxford University Press; New York. 1994.

Delgado, James P. "Operation Crossroads." *American History Illustrated.* May/June 1993, Volume XXVIII, Number 2. Pages 50–59.

Douhet, Giulio. *The Command of the Air.* Translated by Dino Ferrari from the 1927 second edition. Coward McCann Inc.; New York. 1942.

"Dragons and Centipedes at Sea." *Naval Institute Proceedings.* November 1995, pp. 65–69.

Dupuy, Colonel (US Army, Retired) Trevor N. *The Evolution of Weapons and Warfare.* Da Capo Paperback; New York. 1984.

Eastaugh, Steven R. "Financing the Correct Rate of Growth of Medical Technology." *Quarterly Review of Economics and Business*, pp. 54–60, Vol. 30, No. 4, Winter 1990.

Edmonds, Brigadier General Sir James E. *Military Operations: France and Belgium, 1914.* MacMillan and Co. Limited; London. 1933.

Edwards, Major John E. *Combat Service Support Guide.* Stackpole Books; Harrisburg, Pennsylvania. 1989.

Eller, Rear Admiral Ernest McNeill. *The Soviet Sea Challenge.* Cowles Book Company, Inc.; USA. 1971.

Fahey, James C. *The Ship's and Aircraft of the United States Fleet.* Naval Institute Press; Annapolis Maryland. Seventh edition, 1988. (First edition in 1939).

Fiske, Rear Admiral Bradley A. "The Strongest Navy." *Current History.* July 1922, pp. 557–63.

"Forward. . . From the Sea." US Navy and Marine Corps White Paper. Department of the Navy, Washington. 1994.

Freedman, Lawrence, editor. *War*. Oxford University Press; New York. 1994.

". . . From the Sea: Preparing the Naval Service for the 21st Century." US Navy and Marine Corps White Paper. Department of the Navy, Washington. 1992.

Fryer, Captain James W. "Flying With the Bone." *Naval Institute Proceedings*. February 1995, p. 49.

Fukuyama, Francis. *The End of History and the Last Man*. The Free Press; New York. 1992.

Gaddis, John Lewis. *Strategies of Containment: A Critical Appraisal of the Postwar American National Security Policy*. Oxford University Press; New York. 1982.

"Galicia's Atlantic coast basin—A new oil province?" *Oil & Gas Journal: International Petroleum News and Technology*. March 28, 1994, p. 68.

Gansler, Jacques S. *Affording Defense*. The MIT Press; Cambridge, Massachusetts. 1991.

Garcia, Sergeant First Class Elroy. "Modern technology updates the spirit of the Louisiana Maneuvers." *Soldiers*. September 1993, Volume 48, No. 9, pp. 6–7.

Garden, Timothy. *The Technology Trap: Science and the Military*. Brassey's Defence Publishers; New York. 1989.

Gardiner, Robert, editor. *The Earliest Ships: The Evolution of Boats into Ships*. Naval Institute Press; Annapolis, Maryland. 1996.

Gardiner, William Howard. "The Philippines and Sea Power." *North American Review*. August 1922, pp. 165–73.

Gatchel, Theodore L. *At the Water's Edge: Defending against the Modern Amphibious Assault*. Naval Institute Press; Annapolis Maryland. 1996.

Gill, Commander C. C. "The New Far East Doctrine." *Naval Institute Proceedings*. September 1922.

Gray, Colin S. *The Leverage of Sea Power: The Strategic Advantage of Navies in War*. The Free Press; New York. 1992.

Gray, Colin S. "National Styles in Strategy: The American Example." *International Security*. Fall 1981, vol 6, no 2.

Gray, Colin S. *Nuclear Strategy and National Style*. Hamilton Press; Lanham, Md. 1986.

Gray, Colin S. *Weapons Don't Make War: Policy, Strategy, & Military Technology*. University Press of Kansas; Lawrence, Kansas. 1993.

Gretton, Vice-Admiral Sir Peter. *Maritime Strategy: A Study of Defense Problems*. Frederick A. Praeger, Publishers; New York. 1965.

Gromov, Admiral F. N. "The Russian Navy's Commander Responds." *Naval Institute Proceedings*. June 1996.

Hall, Alfred R. *Ballistics in the Seventeenth Century*. Cambridge at the University Press; New York. 1952.

Hart, B. H. Liddell. *Defence of the West.* William Morrow & Co.; New York. 1950.

Hillen, John. "Military Might." *National Review.* June 30, 1997. Vol. XLIX, No. 12, pp. 38–41.

Hoffman, Lieutenant Colonel F. G. "The U.S. Marine Corps in Review," *Naval Institute Proceedings*, May 1997, pp. 90–97.

Holly, Irving B. "Doctrine and Technology as Viewed by Some Seminal Theorists of the Art of Warfare from Clausewitz to the Mid-Twentieth Century." Found in *Emerging Doctrines and Technologies*, 1988, Pfaltzgraff et al, editors.

Hoyt, Edwin P. *Japan's War: The Great Pacific Conflict.* Da Capo Press; New York. 1986.

*Information Please Almanac.* Hughton Mifflin Company; Boston & New York. 1997.

*Jane's Fighting Ships.* Jane's Information Group; United Kingdom. 1919 and 1931 editions.

Janowitz. "The Military Professional." Found in *War*, Lawrence Freedman, editor. Oxford University Press; New York. 1994.

Johnston, Alastair Iain. "Thinking about Strategic Culture." *International Security.* Spring 1995, vol 19, no 4, pp. 32–64.

Kelly, Ensign Patrick M. "The U.S. Navy Must Re-Evaluate Its Doctrine." *Naval Institute Proceedings.* July 1996, pp. 68–69.

Kraul, Chris. "A Spar is Born: Advances Let Oil Firms Go Where No Drill Has Gone Before," *Los Angeles Times*, Monday, February 17, 1997, p. D1.

Kraus, Commander George F. Jr. "Information Warfare in 2015." *Naval Institute Proceedings.* August 1995, p. 42.

Krieger, Joel. *The Oxford Companion to Politics of the World.* Oxford University Press; New York. 1993.

Krulak, General Charles C. "Facing Westward to the Future." *Naval Institute Proceedings.* March 1997, pp. 12–18.

Kutta, Timothy J. "Captain Charles R Samson would not give up on his idea to use a towed barge as an aircraft carrier." *Aviation History.* May 1997, pp. 10 and 62.

"Law of the Sea: The End Game." National Intelligence Council, Richard N. Cooper, Chairman. Published by the United States Government; Washington, DC March 1996.

Lewis, John W. and Xue Litai. *China's Strategic Seapower.* Stanford University Press; Stanford, California. 1994.

Machiavelli, Niccolo. *The Prince.* Translated by George Bull. Penguin Books; London. 1961.

Macris, Lieutenant Jeffrey R. "Is Mahan Relevant?" *Naval Institute Proceedings.* May 1995, pp. 72–76.

Mahan, Captain Alfred Thayer. *The Influence of Sea Power Upon History: 1660–1783*. Dover Publications, Inc.; New York. 1987 (abridged copy of the 1894 fifth edition).

Mahan, Alfred Thayer. *Naval Administration and Warfare: Some General Principals*. Little, Brown, and Company; Boston. 1918.

Mallory, Keith and Arvid Ottar. *The Architecture of War*. Pantheon Books; New York. 1973.

Manigart, Philippe. "Mass Armed Forces in Decline." In *War*, Lawrence Freedman, editor. Oxford University Press; New York. 1994.

Manzagol, Thomas and Eleni Brown. "Where's My Stuff?" *Army Logistician: Professional Bulletin of the United States Army Logistics*. PB 700–96–3. May-June 1996.

Marcus, G. J. *A Naval History of England: The Formative Centuries*. Little, Brown and Company; Boston. 1961.

Martin, Laurence W. *The Sea in Modern Strategy*. Frederick A. Praeger, Publishers; New York. Published for The Institute for Strategic Studies. 1967.

Miers, John H. "Technology Gives Gulf Prospects World-Class Investment Appeal," *Oil & Gas Journal*, January 20, 1997, pp. 50–56.

*The Military Balance*. London Institute for Strategic Studies; London. Annual: 1963–1997.

Murray, Williamson. *Strategy for Defeat: The Luftwaffe 1933–1945*. Air University Press; Alabama. 1983.

"Naval Rivalry." *Jane's Intelligence Review*, Special Report No. 7, *Trouble in Paradise: Maritime Risks and Threats in the Western Pacific*. Pp. 17–23. Jane's Information Group, Ltd; London. 1995.

"New Weapons of War: As it searches for a mission, the Army uses computers to stretch money." *U.S. News & World Report*. May 31, 1993, pp. 30–33.

Nye, Joseph S., Jr. and William A. Owens. "America's Information Edge." *Foreign Affairs*. March/April 1996, vol 75, no 2, pp. 20–36.

"Oil giants tap Gulf depths: New technology opens a field of their dreams," *Sacramento Bee*, Tuesday, April 30, 1996, p. C1.

Oppenheimer, J. Robert. *Uncommon Sense*. (This is a collection of essays compiled after Oppenheimer's death in 1967. N. Metropolis, Gian-Carlo Rota, and David Sharp, editors.) Birkhauser; Boston. 1984.

"Operation Crossroads." *American History Illustrated*. May/June 1993.

*Operation Crossroads: The Official Pictorial Record*. The Office of the Historian, Joint Task Force One. Wm. H. Wise & Co., Inc.; New York. 1946.

Parker, Commander Thomas A. "The Navy Got It: Desert Storm's Wake-Up Call." *Naval Institute Proceedings*. September 1994, pp. 33–36.

Paret, Peter, editor. *Makers of Modern Strategy From Machiavelli to the Nuclear Age*. Princeton University Press; Princeton, New Jersey. 1986.

Pasquarette, Captain James F. and Colonel William G. Foster. "An Army Heavy Brigade Goes Afloat." *Naval Institute Proceedings*. May 1994, pp. 89–92.

Pendley, William T. "The U.S. Navy, Forward Defense, and the AirLand Battle." Found in *Emerging Doctrines and Technologies*, 1988, Pfaltzgraff et al, editors.

Pfaltzgraff, Robert L. et al. *Emerging Doctrines and Technologies: Implications for Global and Regional Political-Military Balances*. Lexington Books; Lexington, Massachusetts. 1988.

Pipes, Richard. "Why the Soviet Union Thinks It Could Fight and Win a Nuclear War." *Commentary*. July 1977, vol 64, no 1, pp. 21–34.

"Piracy: back in vogue with a vengeance." *Jane's Intelligence Review*, Special Report No. 7, *Trouble in Paradise: Maritime Risks and Threats in the Western Pacific*, p. 7. Jane's Information Group, Ltd; London. 1995.

Pirages, Dennis. *Global Technopolitics: The International Politics of Technology and Resources*. Brooks/Cole Publishing Company; Pacific Grove, California. 1989.

"Potential of Pacific frontiers of former Soviet oil, gas empire." *Oil & Gas Journal: International Petroleum News and Technology*. April 25, 1994, p. 69.

Potter, E. B. *Sea Power: A Naval History*. Naval Institute Press; Annapolis, Maryland. 1984.

Rasler, Karen and William R. Thompson. "Technological Innovation, Capability Positional Shifts, and Systemic War." *The Journal of Conflict Resolution*, September 1991, Volume 35, Number 3.

"Reaching Globally, Reaching Powerfully: The United States Air Force in the Gulf War." September 1991.

Robb, Izetta Winter. "Navy's First Ace," pp. 82–83. Found in Adrian O. Van Wyen's *Naval Aviation in World War I*. Published by the Chief of Naval Operations, U.S. Government Printing Office; Washington, DC 1969.

Rogers, Lieutenant William J. "Toward a Doctrine of U.S. Naval Power." *Naval Institute Proceedings*. December 1996, pp. 58–60.

Rosen, Stephen Peter. "New Ways of War: Understanding Military Innovation." *International Security*. Summer 1988, vol 13, no 1, pp. 134–168.

Rosen, Stephen Peter. "Military Effectiveness: Why Society Matters." *International Security*. Spring 1995, vol 19, no 4, pp. 5–31.

Rosen, Stephen Peter. *Winning the Next War: Innovation and the Modern Military*. Cornell University Press; Ithaca and London. 1991.

Rowny, Ambassador Edward L. "Strategic Offense-Defense Mixes: The Impact of Arms Control." Found in *Emerging Doctrines and Technologies*, 1988, Pfaltzgraff et al, editors.

"Sea delivery: a rogue state's third option." *Jane's Intelligence Review*. May 1996, Volume 8, Number 5.

Snow, C. P. *The Two Cultures and A Second Look*. Cambridge University Press; New York. 1987 (part I first published in 1959, Part II first published in 1964).

Southby, Richard and Warren Greenberg, editors. *Health Care Technology under Financial Constraints*. Battelle Press; Columbus, Ohio. 1987.

Stanton, Shelby L. *World War II Order of Battle*. Galagad Books; New York. 1984.

*STAR 21: Strategic Technologies for the Army of the Twenty-first Century*. Prepared by the Board on Army Science and Technology, Commission on Engineering and Technical Systems, National Research Council. National Academy Press; Washington. 1992

*Statistical Abstract of the U.S.: 1995*. 115th Edition. US Bureau of the Census; Washington, DC 1995.

Stern, Robert C. *The Lexington Class Carriers*. Naval Institute Press; Annapolis, Maryland. 1993.

Terraine, John. *The U-Boat Wars: 1916–1945*. G. P. Putnam's Sons; New York. 1989.

Thucydides. *The Peloponnesian War*. Revised with introduction by T. E. Wick. McGraw-Hill, Inc.; New York. 1982.

Till, Geoffrey. *Maritime Strategy and the Nuclear Age*. St. Martin's Press; New York. 1984.

Toffler, Alvin. *The Third Wave*. Little, Brown and Company; New York. 1980.

Toffler, Alvin and Heidi Toffler. *War and Anti-War*. Little, Brown and Company; New York. 1993.

Tritten, James J. "Maneuver Warfare at Sea." *Naval Institute Proceedings*. September 1995, p. 52–54.

*The United States Merchant Marine at War, Report of the War Shipping Administration to the President*. U.S. Printing Office; Washington, DC. 1946.

"U.S. E&P surge hinges on technology, not oil price." *Oil & Gas Journal: International Petroleum News and Technology*. January 13, 1997, p. 42.

Van Creveld, Martin. *Supplying War: Logistics from Wallenstein to Patton*. Cambridge University Press; New York. 1977.

Van Wyen, Adrian O. Historian, Deputy Chief of Naval Operations (Air). *Naval Aviation in World War I*. Published by the Chief of Naval Operations, U.S. Government Printing Office; Washington, DC 1969.

Waltz, Kenneth N. *Theory of International Politics*. McGraw-Hill, Inc.; New York. 1979.

Webster, Sir Charles Kingsly and Noble Frankland. *History of the Second World War.* United Kingdom Military Series, 4 volumes and appendix. H. M. Stationery Office; London.

Webster, Sir Charles Kingsly and Noble Frankland. *The Strategic Air Offensive Against Germany, 1939–1945.* H. M. Stationery Office; London. 1961.

"Why Not 100 Knots." *Naval Institute Proceedings.* November 1996.

Williams, Kathleen Broome. *Secret Weapon: U.S. High-Frequency Direction Finding in the Battle of the Atlantic.* Naval Institute Press; Annapolis, Maryland. 1996.

*The World Factbook: 1995.* Central Intelligence Agency; Washington, D.C. 1995.

Zuckerman, Mortimer B. "Winning the future's wars." *U.S. News & World Report.* May 12, 1997, p. 83.

# Index

For Product Safety Concerns and Information please contact our EU
representative GPSR@taylorandfrancis.com Taylor & Francis Verlag GmbH,
Kaufingerstraße 24, 80331 München, Germany


Printed and bound by CPI Group (UK) Ltd, Croydon, CR0 4YY

08/05/2025

01864406-0008